Been There, Done That:

16 Secrets of Success for Entrepreneurs

Angi Ma Wong

Pacific Heritage Books
Palos Verdes

Also by Angi Ma Wong:

-Night of the Red Moon
-TARGET: The U.S. Asian Market,
A Practical Guide to Doing Business
-The Practical Feng Shui Chart Kit:
A Tool to Chart the Direction of Your Life
-The Wind/Water Wheel:
A Feng Shui Tool for Transforming Your Life

Been There, Done That:
16 Secrets of Success for Entrepreneurs
Published by Pacific Heritage Books
Copyright 1997 by Angi Ma Wong

ISBN-0-9635906-3-4
Library of Congress Catalog Card Number 96-93142
Wong, Angi Ma

Grateful appreciation is extended to Lynne Choy Uyeda, Mike Snell, Randall Lewis, Suzanne Wickham-Beaird, Cynthia Chin-Lee, Tom O'Malia, Ted Vegvari, Pam Gilberd, Marian and Gary Gray, and Steve Liu for their inspiration and support.

Cover by Sammy Loh
Printed in the United States of America by Gilliland Printing

To all who have found the courage to take the first step

and

*to Norman, my husband and best friend, with whom I have
traveled the journey of life and entrepreneurship together*

Foreword

Life is a journey. Entrepreneurship is a passion. An entrepreneurial life is a passionate journey. Too often writers and educators attempt to explain entrepreneurship as a process. They seek to reduce it to a formula: a connect-the-dots approach that if followed per their suggested sequence, will result in success. Nothing is further from the truth.

Entrepreneurs are about loving their journey, not their destination. They are about creating, not managing. And above all, they are about making their own choices. The price they pay for these apparent luxuries are rejection, failure, and at times, the worst of all banishment, "I told you so."

But they continue. They are driven. They seek only to control their own destinies. Doing that makes the journey exciting and satisfying.

Answering why they venture is only the first question. The real challenge is how do they do it? How can so many companies fail every day while the popular press and our own circle of friends and associates tell of new, successful ventures being launched daily? What are the secrets of these marvelous people we honor with the title of *entrepreneur*?

In **Been There, Done That**: *16 Secrets of Success for Entrepreneurs*, Angi Ma Wong opens the door of her journey and shares her inner thoughts of the life of an entrepreneur. Uniquely structured as a combination of secrets that both led and sustained her journey, she paints a realistic picture of the emotion and skill set needed to first survive, and then succeed.

Recognizing the difference between managing and creating, the difference between starting and evolving, the difference between testing and committing all energy, the difference between listening and presenting to your market, are all secrets known to and shared by entrepreneurs. Now they have been exposed to all who feel they have the courage for this, the most passionate journey of their lives.

Tom O'Malia
Director, The Entrepreneur Program
University of Southern California

Table of Contents

The Dreams Come First

SECRET NUMBER 1

Vision

**When you look back on your life,
you will regret the things you haven't
done more than those you did.**
-H. Jackson Brown

Dear Friends and Family,

I am writing to you because many of you may think that Angi Wong has dropped off the face of the earth as you have not heard from me in some time and I haven't had time to call.

Please forgive this impersonal method of communicating with you all but by the time you receive this letter, I will have had my lymph node surgery under my right arm and will be unable to type, drive, write, lift, push, pull, etc., etc. for 2-3 weeks. This second surgery follows my first to remove a tumor on June 9. I discovered it, immediately had a mammogram and two needle biopsies which revealed its malignancy. July and August will be spent at home resting and going to daily radiation treatments for 5-7 weeks.

Of course all of this happened while: our new addition is being built with workmen, inspectors and contractor underfoot; worrying about my cousin and her husband getting out of China after the Tiananmen Square massacre; my sister-in-law ready to deliver her baby any day; a cousin due for a Cesarean birth (both were girls born exactly a week apart); a close uncle dying in Hong Kong; a girlfriend becoming very ill after a trip, necessitating hospitalization upon her return to the States; another friend asking for my assistance in placing two little girls for adoption (their mother is in a coma, dying of cancer); my mom's high blood pressure; a cousin getting married last Saturday and three East Coast relatives here in town; the dogs got loose and chewed up the approved on-site house plans; the contractor losing his $10,000 check we gave him; two earthquakes here in L. A.; Jason graduating from junior high school this Thursday and my dad not well—all in a normal week in my life!

I couldn't imagine what else could happen until I opened my mail today and found that I had been called for jury duty again! All the above has happened only in the last two weeks!   I don't believe I've ever had fourteen days of such emotional stress, anxiety, and excitement--most of which I could do without.

Anyway, I am fine as I insisted on this week of "normalcy" by going back to work and tying up all my loose ends there as I take the summer off to rest. I think all of this is God's way of telling me to take it easy so I can enjoy my garden. Of course the children will be off for the summer beginning next week so there goes the rest...

More later,
Angi

Almost eight years ago when my family and friends received the letter I sent in June of 1989, one called back and told me, "I didn't know whether to laugh or cry. It was like something dark from Erma Bombeck." Unluckily for me, things got worse and my life disintegrated into chaos during my three months from hell. Several days before I went in for my first chemotherapy treatment, I received the news that my two-year-old nephew had been killed in the Sioux City, Iowa, airplane crash. A week later, two of my children and I boarded a plane for a ten-day trip to Hawaii and never before had I never felt such panic about flying as I did then.

Nine chemotherapy treatments had been scheduled for me, beginning on July 21, three weeks apart. The first four weren't bad, resulting in a little bit of nausea and a sore arm. As a matter of fact, I felt better after each 45-minute IV drip session and thought, "This is a piece of cake." Boy, was I in for a surprise.

Knowing that my family and I were planning a three-week trip to Asia during Christmas, my oncologist increased the dosages in order to decrease the number of treatments to seven. To make a long story short, it was awful. I was nauseous and lost my appetite for three days after the fifth, sixth, and last visits.

Barely had I recovered, I found myself frantically Christmas shopping for all my relatives and friends during the week before our departure. The eight of us—Mom, Dad, my husband Norman, our children Jason, Wendy, Jamie, Steve, and I flew to Hong Kong for our long-anticipated vacation.

Frankly, I didn't want to go. Physically and emotionally, I was a wreck, and quite honestly, when we got there, I overdid things. Our days began around ten in the morning when the stores opened and ended after dinner with friends and family each night after 10 p.m. We shopped 'til we dropped, not getting enough rest, rushing around, trying to accommodate everyone's needs and desires as well as do and see everything.   It was a real mistake.

Two days after my return to the States, I was feeling so bizarre physically that I knew that I wasn't suffering from a case of garden-variety jet lag. My heart was pounding and I was overcome with morbid thoughts of death, dying, and a sense of doom. Those of you who know will recognize these as classic symptoms of panic attacks.

A visit to my doctor confirmed the worst. I was suffering from depression brought on by a hormonal imbalance, caused by the chemo. Rest and recuperate, he ordered, sending me into therapy. And so it was that for the first time in my entire adult life, I had leisure time.   Because I couldn't read or watch television due to a temporary inability to concentrate, I could only work on my garden, sit in the sunshine by the pool, cook one meal a day, give an occasional speech, and visit with friends.

And my life was changed forever.

———

I hope that you did not have to experience a life-threatening illness or other trauma as I did to compel you to start your own business.   There are numerous quality books and publications available in bookstores, from federal, state, and local governments and community organizations on the technical and practical aspects of a business start-up. Most are technical, step-by-step manuals on how to go about it, sprinkled liberally with solid advice and legalese. Although I will provide you with a business plan outline in the appendix of this book to get you thinking and started, **Been There, Done Tha**t: *16 Secrets of an Entrepreneur* is not one of those publications.

Many of you will go into business for yourself with the goal of making a lot of money. This is a major mistake. As the Chinese say: Simple to open shop. Another thing to keep it open. The biggest profits mean the gravest risks. Money should be the by-product, not your goal. Confucius sagely told us 2,500 years ago: If your love your job, you will never work a day in your life. Nor should you become self-employed because you are excellent at what you do technically and think that you will succeed wildly as an entrepreneur. You will then become as Michael Gerber describes it: "a technician suffering from an entrepreneurial seizure."

This book is about liberation and empowerment. It is about freedom and choices, and taking responsibility for those choices. It is about self-discipline, self-reliance, hard work, being organized and frugal, creative and resourceful. Most of all, it is about you, what you really care about, your values, and what you want out of life. Each one of us has the seed of entrepreneurship inside of us. For some, it will develop naturally and easily. For others, especially those who are technically and analytically-inclined, mostly left-brained folks, it will require a completely different way of thinking and doing things...shifts in your paradigms.

Been There, Done That: *16 Secrets of an Entrepreneur* is for those of you who have always dreamed of starting and owning a business, being your own boss, and who, in my workshops, wanted to know more about what it took to be a successful entrepreneur. I wish I had a book like this when I started. Some of the lessons are my own hard-earned ones. Others are the words of friends, family, supportive or famous people, and yes, even, strangers, that I found inspirational or helpful along the way.

Think of the book as a set of notes from someone who has taken the class that you have just registered for. You can learn from my mistakes and actuate your own dreams. In your heart you know that being an entrepreneur has nothing to with power, prestige, or money, but about living a life that is true to your own values and dreams. True entrepreneurship should stimulate your personal and professional growth. It should cause you to stretch your mind, body, and spirit.

The good news is that it means getting up every morning knowing that you are in control of everything related to your business, for better or worse. The bad news is that you may eat, drink, sleep, and think about it, both in your conscious and subconscious, twenty-four hours a day. Moreover, you have to decide what your definition of success is, and what price you are you willing to pay to be successful.

My price was too high, I regret to say, and I am trying very hard to rectify the neglect of my children during a time when they needed me, a time that perhaps, like yours, coincided with the building of my businesses. What will your price be? Will you be willing to pay it? Jacqueline Kennedy Onassis is attributed with saying, "If you screw up raising your kids, nothing much else you do in life matters."

So timing is important. Parents, make time for your children by staying at home with them when they are young, in school, at home, and need you, while you dream and plan. As they become more independent and need you less to be involved in their activities (usually around pre-adolescence when their peers become all-important in their lives.)

There is a significant difference in the quality and kind of time you must give to your K through 8 children compared to what your high schooler or college student needs. Be wise, know the difference, and make your choices accordingly. Understand also that those small, day-to-day choices may not be easy or right, but as a part of the big picture, they will not be disastrous!

You have probably heard the daunting statistics: Each year there are a million business start-ups in the United States alone. Eighty percent of those will fail within the first five years. Of those that survive, another eighty percent will not survive during the second five years. *Hello*, it's reality check time, and welcome to the exciting, challenging world of the entrepreneur where an MBA from a top business school may be a disadvantage and where not knowing anything about starting, owning, and running a business may be the best thing going for you.

An ancient Japanese saying goes like this: "To know ten things, learn one." You will learn many things as you embark on this adventure and grow wise en route. Always keep in mind that life is a journey, not a destination. It will be important to trust your instincts as only you know what is best and right for you.

Having cancer was a wake-up call for me. I saw it as a sign from God to stop and smell the roses. Although my life was wonderful, thank you—great husband, fantastic kids, loving family, good job with benefits, something was missing. As I was stopping to smell, plant, and water the roses during that summer of 1989, I made some important discoveries. The forced inactivity made me think about life in general, how precious it was and when it came down to it, what my true priorities were. I became disinterested in and wanted to get rid of most of my material possessions, unclutter my life, do the things I had been putting off, and most importantly, hold my family and friends closely to me, both literally and figuratively speaking.

It was during that hiatus that I also made a conscious, deliberate choice not to be swept along any longer like a piece of flotsam in the rushing river of life. I was going to *be* that river: active, dynamic, powerful, proactive, and in charge. "Lead, follow, or get outta the way" became my motto.

All my working life I have been involved in education—as a junior high school and adult education teacher, counselor, job developer, and administrator with the Los Angeles Unified School District. Perhaps I was going through my midlife crisis, prematurely brought on by my cancer. All I know was that I found myself asking, "Isn't there more to life than this?" Some of you may have been feeling the same niggling discontent, reached the glass ceiling in your company, or perhaps have been laid off from your job. Perhaps, like me, you're a baby boomer, and your children require less of your time and attention, or maybe you're just ready to do things and live your life differently. They don't call it "change of life" for nothing, you know.

Some of you may have been thrust into business that already exists, or perhaps you are moving into a position vacated by someone else. You may feel a bit overwhelmed about filling that person's shoes and my advice is don't even try. Move that other man or woman's footwear aside and blaze your own path, in your own shoes, in your own style, and at your own pace.

Do you think that dying people tell themselves that they wish they had spent more time at the office? More likely, they feel a sense of regret, sadness, and loss for all the things they put off doing...*when* I have the time, *when* the business makes more money, *when* the kids are grown, *when* I retire. Wake up, folks, the time to realize your dreams is now and today.

What will *you* regret not doing if you found out today that you only had a year, six months, a week, or a day left to live? Think about it. You could die today and your dreams will never be realized. Don't wait for your wake-up call, the discovery of cancer, a heart attack, stroke, the loss of a spouse, divorce, or an automobile accident. The time to do it is now, even if it is just to get a notebook and start making a list of all the things you want to do in your life. As Dr. Toni Grant says, "Life is not a dress rehearsal."

Just the other day I read this message on the back of a teenager's T-shirt: There are two kinds of people in the world. Those who make things happen and those who wish they did. Which are you?

A woman who sat next to me at a meeting glanced over at my open monthly appointment calendar and remarked in awe, "You have such an exciting and interesting life." I turned, looked her straight in the eye and said, "You can too." Your life is what you make it. Be a participant, not a spectator and take the first step today.

Don't be one of those people who looks back on life and regrets all the things you didn't do. You have freedom and you have choice. And you are living in the one country in the whole world in which new ideas and companies can germinate and flourish, unencumbered by dusty traditions and stifling political or cultural environments and attitudes.

To use all the cliches: Today is the first day of the rest of your life. A journey of a thousand miles begins with the first step. Yesterday is history. Tomorrow is a mystery. We only have today and that's why it's called the present. Corny, but true. If you can't climb the ladder of success, build a new ladder. Go for it, kiddo. The time is now.

What in the heck are you waiting for?

SECRET NUMBER 2

mission

Believe in what you do.
Do what you believe in.
-1993 Rotary International Theme

While I had always thought about having my own business and explored several possibilities, it was not until I lapsed into depression brought on by chemotherapy, that I thought about it seriously. As I sat in the serene beauty of my garden, listening to the birds singing and the gentle swoosh of distant traffic, I reflected on the many paths that I had traveled to reach that moment.

Perhaps you too, will have or have had a similar revelation, or it may have come to you through years of self-development, reflection and discovery. It matters not how, but rather, that it did happen and you join the ranks of those truly blessed ones who, like myself, have discovered what your mission and purpose in life is.

It helps tremendously to know yourself well. Acknowledging and assessing my own background, education, practical skills, interests, strengths, weaknesses, likes, dislikes, and passions, mine came to me in a flash on a sunny day under the peach tree in my back yard.

I loved people, doing things for others for the sheer joy of it, and had a bit of the missionary spirit. My grandparents had inspired me to love and be proud of my community, country and culture. Mom and Dad had instilled the strong Confucian values of hard work, thrift, responsibility, compassion, and duty to family.

But I had the maturity and wisdom to acknowledge that I am not perfect, nor will I ever be. As the first child of two in my family, I could be inflexible, insecure, too serious, a perfectionist, impulsive, and too trusting and naive. Besides, I had math anxieties, and was intolerant of incompetence and inefficiency. My strong points were that I enjoyed public speaking, read voraciously, and had been writing creatively since seventh grade. I wanted to spend more time at home with my four children who were growing up too fast. I was an organized, creative thinker who liked to set goals for myself, work at my own pace, and so on.

Actually, I took the first step in my journey to entrepreneurship years ago. When I arrived in Los Angeles as a new bride in 1967, my husband and I moved into an apartment near the University of Southern California, just fifteen minutes away from Chinatown. At that time there was only one large Chinese market there from which we could purchase the familiar vegetables, fruits, and canned, bottled, and cellophane-wrapped staples of a Chinese kitchen. Often we would run into friends and relatives at Yee Sing Cheong. It was the emotional home for many of us and making the trek there every several weeks was a way to keep in touch with our culture and community. It was also just about the only place in town at which one could buy tofu, bok choy, and soy sauce.

Now fast forward to 1989. It is two decades later and Asians are emigrating to the United States in record numbers after the repeal of laws that had perpetuated the quota system in place since 1943. Chinese communities have now sprung up in the suburbs of Southern California's San Gabriel Valley. Cities such as Monterey Park, Alhambra, Arcadia, and San Marino are scrambling to adjust to the changes in the population, not without a backlash, resulting in "English-only" campaigns and other politically incorrect activities.

By now you could get everything from kim chee to sushi, long beans to short-grain rice, and ten different kinds of soy sauce made by ten different companies in the many local grocery stores. And the Asian food sections in American supermarkets have expanded in size from one shelf to *aisles* as East begins to meet mainstream West.

Old homes in established neighborhoods are being torn down and replaced by "monster" homes built by new immigrants. Trees are removed and mini-malls are springing up like weeds at numerous intersections. Home prices skyrocket and there is a buying frenzy as everyone, Asians and non-Asians alike, rush to buy, buy, buy into the American dream of home ownership.

Then the booming housing market crashes and when the dust settles, developers make a remarkable discovery. It seemed that the only people who are buying during the California recession that began in 1990 are of Asian heritage. It was purely coincidental that it was at this time that I was recovering from my chemotherapy-induced depression and was determined to start my own business.

I had experienced and observed those demographic changes through the years and thought about non-Asians who had grown up all over the country with British and European roots and Judeo-Christian values. They were stumped as to how to go about conducting business and developing social, familial, and business relationships with this burgeoning new minority and needed assistance. After all, I figured, there were a lot of opportunities for intercultural miscommunication and misunderstanding. And that's when the proverbial light bulb went on in my head. I would parlay my life's experiences into a service to help those folks who needed guidance in these areas.

With about $300 invested in business cards and stationeryI coined the title of "intercultural consultant," and having taken that first step of my thousand-mile journey, I was on my way. No accounting or business courses. (Not advisable.) No experience. (Not advisable.) No office or clients. My husband Norman still marvels at my chutzpah to launch out on my own as I did. I had never facilitated any trans-Pacific business deals or even knew anything about business. But I had courage and had acquired outstanding human relations skills acquired as a diplomat and restaurateur's daughter and a sincere desire to help people. And I had a vision that could be summed up thus, "Bridging cultures for better business."

Michael Gerber, author of *The E-Myth,* challenges all of us who wish to become entrepreneurs with this: What do you want your business to look like, five or ten years from now? I envisioned myself as a sharply-dressed businesswoman, attending meetings to ascertain the needs of my clients, travelling across the United States giving speeches, advising my audiences on how to strategize, sell and market to Asians in a culturally-sensitive way, conducting interesting and practical training seminars, and generally being a creative problem solver for my clients. My happy family of six would enjoy a comfortable home in a great community and we would all benefit from my success.

I knew that promotion and marketing were critical to my success and to gain visibility, I gave free speeches to local organizations and at every chance, distributed my business cards. More often than not, I had to explain to people what an intercultural consultant was and did, but this small inconvenience did not deter me from my vision or mission. During a short period of time, I had spoken before both the Palos Verdes Peninsula Chamber of Commerce and at the inaugural meeting of the Palos Verdes Sunset Rotary Club. My "sing-for-my-supper" speech was a concise but lively and practical presentation entitled, "ABC: Asian Business Communication, From Head to Toe." My presentation offered about a dozen tips on how to communicate non-verbally while conducting business with Asians.

I got a call from one person who had heard me speak on both occasions called me up.

"Angi," Brooks Roddan asked, "would you be interested in speaking on a panel at a building conference? No money, but you'll get a lot of exposure," he added.

I realized immediately that it was just the opportunity I had been waiting for: the chance to reach a larger, more diverse audience and potential clients, so I accepted. As a lifelong writer and former English major who had excelled in the one public speaking course I took at Virginia Tech, I knew that giving speeches was much like Chinese cooking: 95 percent preparation and 5 percent presentation, at the podium or at the stove. The topic was "Appealing to the Asian Homebuyer," and after a lot of thought and research, I had prepared twenty minutes of remarks and spent hours hand lettering my flip charts.

My first "real" audience only had about 60-70 attendees, but afterwards, several people came up to me to chat. One was Roger AndersonVice President of Sales and Marketing for one of the largest developers on the West Coast, Lewis Homes, Inc.

I'll never forget his words.

"I was the most impressed with you," he told me, "all I want to know is how much do you charge and when can you come out to train our people?"

It was the beginning of the greatest adventure of my life which continues today—exciting, enriching, liberating, joyous, frustrating, and simply wonderful. By the time I had been in business over seven years, word-of-mouth had expanded my clientele to include over 300 major commercial and residential developers, architectural and interior design firms, loan, financial, and escrow institutions. That number did not include the non-building industries.

I had found my mission and began to carve my niche.

Now it's *your* turn. Make the decision not to waste another day dreaming of the person you want to be now that you have your self-knowledge and vision. Begin right away to use the talents and gifts that you have to realize those dreams. Ingrid , Ingrid's words remind us: "I've never sought success in order to get fame and money; it's the talent and the passion that count in success."

To dream of the person you would like to be is to waste the person you are. Don't waste the person you are, but rather, make your dreams into reality with the qualities you already possess: honesty, integrity, character, diligence, the work ethic, and loyalty to your family and country.

Ecclisiastes 3:1 reminds us: "To every thing there is a season and a time to every purpose under the heaven." If you have looked into your heart and at your life and decided that this *is* your season to pursue your purpose, so be it. Start now.

SECRET NUMBER 3

Passion

Whatever you can do or think you can do, begin it. Boldness has genius, power, and magic in it.

-Goethe

No guts, no glory. No pain, no gain. No risk, no reward. No responsibility, no credit. Finding *your* own niche is an ongoing process of learning, stretching and growing.

My husband Norman and I considered many different businesses before I happened upon the consulting and publishing that I am involved in now.

We both liked children, so we investigated buying and operating a child-care center. He was enthusiastic; I was not. I had left the teaching profession to stay home to be with our four young children and was ready to move on and out into the adult world again. Quite honestly, I did not relish looking after other people's youngsters day in and day out, coping with the challenges of child-rearing all over again. More importantly, I guess I was feeling a bit paranoid as the McMartin pre-school case was just breaking at that time. I could envision all sorts of scary scenarios. Irate mothers suffering from bad hair days could very well bring us to financial ruin or wreck our reputations. An innocent hug could be misconstrued. Besides, my teaching credential was in secondary and adult education. It was not for me.

On the other hand, I was enamored with the idea of a printing business. Desktop publishing was just taking off at the time and I enjoyed doing layout, writing, and other related activities. Being the copy editor and later the two-time editor-in-chief of Virginia Tech's yearbook *The Bugle* had given me extracurricular skills that I enjoyed using. I truly believed that I could make a go of it, but Norman was the one who balked on that one.

Being a service business that had to deal with customers on a daily basis, meeting their deadlines, coping with their egos and personalities was not the best line of business for me, or us. Looking back, he was absolutely right, of course, just as he has been on so many things. A close friend of ours owns a printing franchise and just in the course of my taking my business there, I have seen the challenges he faces.

Some time ago, I asked my teenaged children if they would do a job they hated if it paid well. The responses among them were varied, and then one summer, the test came.

Two neighbors hired my younger daughter Jamie to babysit their children during the summer. She took the job and enjoyed the income it brought as well as the material things she could buy with her own money. Every day she looked after the youngsters, playing with them, walking their dogs, and entertaining them for two months.

One day, Jamie had an appointment and her older sister Wendy had to substitute for her. When the day was over, Wendy was glad to give the job back. Even for the money, she couldn't tolerate it for a second day.

The point is that you should do what you love. No amount of money can compensate for a business in which you have marginal interest. You may become a millionaire, but you will not feel joyous and most likely will come to hate what you are doing. To be an entrepreneur, interest isn't enough. You must feel *passionate* about what you have chosen.

"Know thyself," advised Socrates. You must know who you are and what makes you happy. Take an interest assessment survey at the counseling office of a local adult school, college or university, or at a career center. You may be pleasantly surprised as you discover new opportunities that are open to you. Today there are a myriad of opportunities that did not exist one, three, five, or ten years ago.

Surveys of this type ask for your responses to basic questions such: "Do you like working indoors or outdoors?" "Do you prefer to be around other people?" "Do you need supervision or are you self -directed?" "Can you set goals for yourself?" And so forth.

I remember a man I met at the Long Beach Naval Shipyard in the course of my outreach efforts for the Division of Adult and Career Education for the Los Angeles Unified School District. He had been a welder for over fourteen years and drove over to the Harbor Occupational Center where I took him to the assessment center for an interest survey. The results indicated that he had artistic abilities and when he discovered that we had an advertising design class, the man became very interested in visiting the class.

It isn't difficult for me to stay humble. Any time I'm feeling too cocky, all I have to do is walk into a computer or electronics superstore and I am put soundly in my place. But I also know that I can stand up in front of an audience of three thousand people and deliver a good speech. What do you do well? What could you share? Start with what you already know and expand outward.

Can you describe your business in ten words or less? I believed that I could make a small difference in the world by bringing people and their cultures together. I felt certain that I had the necessary skills to do this. The concept was a simple one and the basis for my business. "Bridging cultures for better business between Asians and non-Asians" became my slogan and said it all in a nutshell. Within four seconds, I am able to describe the essence of the intercultural services that I provide.

What is the idea for your new business? It could be something very simple, new, or just an improvement on an old idea. Will it be a product or a service? Many of the most successful inventions and businesses are based on very simple concepts. Think of those that are so much a part of our lives today: overnight delivery, a theme park built on the child in all of us, a scrap of paper that sticks temporarily to another surface, tiny hooks that attach themselves to a strip of fuzz, balloon art, multi-level marketing, franchises, plastic storage containers, home parties to sell housewares, cosmetics, and, lingerie, singing telegrams, party and equipment rentals, fast-service and take-out food. These are just a few and I'm sure you can think of many more.

Having imagination is another one of the most important characteristics of being an entrepreneur. Even Albert Einstein said: "Imagination is more important than knowledge." In today's age of technology and information, you can always acquire knowledge, but without imagination and creativity, there will be no spark to ignite your venture.

Ordinary people like you and me can do some serious thinking and honest self analysis to ascertain what our mission in life is. Then we can become empowered to do extraordinary things. We *all* have the potential to be one of these people.

Do you have what it takes to succeed in your own business? I keep this following list tacked to my bulletin board. It was an unsolicited marketing brochure that came with my mail, in other words, junk mail. These traits were those deemed necessary for entrepreneurial success:

1. An eye for opportunity
2. An appetite for hard work
3. Discipline
4. Independence
5. Self-confidence
6. Adaptability
7. Judgement
8. An ability to tolerate stress
9. Need to achieve
10. A focus on profits
11. Self-awareness

The Hagberg Consulting Group compiled a list of traits of 400 entrepreneurs and 1,600 corporate executives and found that few had the right leadership stuff for the long run. It appeared that the very qualities they possessed that had contributed to success were those that hindered them when most of them hit $25 to $40 million in sales.

These ten characteristics were:

1. Acting without deliberation/impulsive
2. Being focused/steadfast
3. Having a positive outlook
4. Opinionated/quick to judge
5. Impatient
6. Preference for simple solutions
7. Autonomous/independent
8. Aggressive
9. Emotionally aloof
10. Risktaker

Data: Hagberg Consulting Group Source: Business Week

According to Hagberg, if you have all of these traits, your start-up will be successful; six, it'll do okay; less than five, you'll best stay with your present job in corporate America.

But timing is important too. You and your ideas may be revolutionary or before their time. Society, the market, attitudes, and political climate may not be conducive to the development or implementation of your idea. What is right is not always popular. What is popular is not always right.

Two friends of mine are examples of this. One came up with the idea of being a financial planner over fifteen years ago; the other was the first to see the need and establish the first video tape library that provided stock footage to whomever needed it. Today, financial planners are a dime a dozen and in the Los Angeles area alone, there are over four hundred video libraries.

Your self-evaluation is a crucial component of becoming an entrepreneur. Without looking at the person you are and knowing what your values and passions are in life, you will ultimately be either unhappy, unsuccessful, or both. If you don't know where you are, how do you know where you are going? If you don't know where you are going, anywhere will do. That anywhere might, with luck, be somewhere, but more likely to be nowhere. Meanwhile, you have spent a lot of time, money, and effort to be nowhere. Think about it.

It does take courage and maturity to look at yourself squarely in the eye while looking in the mirror and into your heart. Take stock and compile a list of all the things that you like doing, that make you happy, and that you do well and most importantly, your values and good traits. These are your strengths. On another list make a list of things that you hate doing, your pet peeves, and your weaknesses. Take a good, hard look at both and you will see a portrait of yourself.

The truer these lists are, the stronger the base upon which you will build your business, and ultimately, your life and your future. Now cover up the list of your weaknesses and focus on all of your good qualities and your strengths. This is the cement for the foundation so crucial to your success. But remember that you had to first identify all the ingredients for the right mix before you could toss out those that would weaken the recipe.

Ask yourself everything and put the answers on the list. The answers tell a lot about who and what you are. Simple questions need to be addressed, such as:

- Do you like working alone or with people?

- Do you like to create things? If so, in what medium? Is it music, writing, fine, graphic or performing arts?
- Are you an analytical left-brain thinker or a intuitive, feeling right-brainer?
- Do you like working with numbers, facts, people, computers, mechanical or organic things, or animals?
- Do you have religious convictions
- Do you feel passionate about something?
- What is it and how can you parlay that passion into a profitable business?
- Do you like doing something that someone else hates to or doesn't have the time to do?
- Are you detail-oriented or view the world by looking at the big picture?
- Do you enjoy dealing with the public or prefer working alone?
- Do enjoy travelling, moving around, changing your environment, or like going to work in the same place every day?
- Are you most comfortable working indoors or outdoors?
- Do you like being around children, the physically challenged, older folks, or a mix of people?
- Have you ever been involved with a business before?
- Do you thrive on order or are energized by disorder and chaos?
- Do you love being in the spotlight and crave being at the center of attention and adulation, or are you satisfied with just knowing that your work behind the scenes is contributing to something?

Then there are issues of how being your own boss will affect those close to you:

- Do all of your family members support the idea of your being your own boss?
- How will a business start-up impact the family, financially, mentally, and psychologically?
- Will they be able to tolerate the quirkiness of having a business operate from out of our home?
- What hours will you be dedicating to the business and to the family?
- Can you count on your significant other for business advice or will that person not be involved in any way?
- Will the younger family members be a part of the business? In what capacities?
- Does everyone in your household understand and accept the changes that will take place?
- Will your home office be depriving the family of useful space?
- Is everyone "going along with the program?"
- Does everyone understand how the rewards and risks, pitfalls and profits will affect them?
- Will your family benefit as a whole from this venture, or will it cause friction and unhappiness?
- What risks and sacrifices are you willing to make? Family time? Health? Friendships? Financial? Emotional? Other?

The list should be candid and excruciatingly honest. Consider it a major reality check before you proceed. Ask yourself what other parts to the entrepreneurial equation are missing from the list? As your heart thumps with excitement and anticipation, and you are ready to take off, taking the time to go through this exercise may help you to avoid heartache and heartbreak down the line.

You simply must discuss all these matters with your entire family so each member is totally aware of and involved in your decision. They need to know how it will affect their lives, both in the short and long term. Ask for and consider their concerns, comments, and suggestions. Don't be surprised at how candid, insightful and truthful their responses may be. Do take what they say very seriously but not personally. They may be providing you with the most valuable feedback you will ever get and even prevent you from making a big mistake in your and their lives.

Remember that being an entrepreneur should *give* you more life, not take away from it.

Gearing Up

SECRET NUMBER 4

Preparation

Do your homework.
-Mom and Dad

Nag, nag, nag. No TV until your homework's done. Remember when? Mom and Dad were right. After vision, passion, and imagination, preparation is the fourth secret to your success as an entrepreneur.

DO YOUR HOMEWORK. Homework for businesses is broken down into three major areas: demographics, psychographics, and geographics. Do you know who your market or customer is today? Who will your market or customer be a year from now? Three years from now? Five years from now? In-depth research provides the answers as well as the means by which to determine whether your business can or will grow.

Demographics are the *who* of a population, their incomes, movement, professions, education, and other vital characteristics and statistics about them. Pick up a copy of the invaluable **American Demographics** magazine and you can look into the crystal ball of the future. The numbers can give you insight on trends and stimulate your imagination about possible business opportunities.

An example of demography in action is the movement of the Baby Boomer generation through the general population of the United States. 77 million babies were born after World War

II during the years 1946 and 1964. This one generation has already redefined America's economy and culture and will continue to drive the trends well into the next century. As the Boomers age, their goals, finances, families, interests, recreational activities, health needs, consumer and voting habits, and many other aspects of their lives will continue to influence our country in many ways.

Psychographics teaches us about the reasons *why* people buy products and services. Consumer behavior in general can be linked to fulfilling psychological needs such as prestige, recognition, power, appreciation, security, convenience, etc. Knowing these motivations empowers you and your business as you can then focus your marketing efforts and selling strategies, thus increasing their effectiveness.

Geographics provides you with the information about *where* people are buying what. Much of this knowledge is season-related; some culture-specific; and some is income-dependent.

You may use a combination of research methods and all will be valid. Personal observation is my favorite as it was what led me to starting my first business as an intercultural consultant. Seeing many donut shops in your community may give you the impression that there is a great market for them and that they are profitable. But then, on the other hand, you may have too much competition. Open up a bagel shop or a low-fat, low-sugar bakery instead!

Some time ago, I was driving to a speaking engagement which took me down a major thoroughfare in Orange County, California. I had to drop by my friend's house for a quick visit en route and wanted to purchase some flowers. Miles and miles passed after I left the freeway and there was not one florist in sight. A possible business start-up there, I remember thinking at the time.

On a recent business flight, I noticed the stewardess putting all of the empty drink cans into a large plastic bag.

"I'm glad to see that your airline recycles," I told her.

"Oh, but we don't, and really should," she corrected me, "there are so many cans from the hundreds of flights out of Houston alone." There again was another business opportunity for somebody.

Most of the information you need is free. Thanks to good old Benjamin Franklin's imagination, our country has over 30,000 libraries now. Your general reference librarian and the computer are your best friends, directing you to the right places at which to do your research. Magazines, newspapers, and other timely publications will keep you abreast of what's current and happening in every possible profession. Books and reference materials cover details of starting and developing a business. Don't overlook material that is published by associations, organizations, institutes, universities, and other non-governmental agencies.

Federal, state, regional, local governments and commissions are another low-cost source of economic information. Our taxes pay for both research and the printing of newsletters, reports, publications, and a wealth of other data. The U.S. government's Small Business Administration has a broad range of assistance programs designed to help folks like you and me. Waiting in the wings is SCORE, the Service Corps of Retired

Executives, which is comprised of men and women who have been successful business owners or executives in various companies.   One-on-one counseling and group training workshops are available to budding entrepreneurs such as you.

Your local and regional chambers of commerce are other great places to get information about your community. Make it a point to join one near you as they usually have the scuttlebutt about incoming businesses and legislation before the general population. Take part in their activities for valuable networking opportunities. Even your stationery supplier such as Office Depot publishes newsletters with many helpful guidelines and hints. And what you may consider as junk mail may have some useful offers, information on seminars and classes, and other resource material.

I found my banking institutions to be a good source of help. These days, competition is fierce to get your business and knowledgeable bank staffers are a definite ally to have on your side as you begin your endeavor. You must establish a good relationship with a local bank and its staff. When people smile at you, greet you by your name, and answer your dumbest questions, you'll feel that you have their support. Because I use the night deposit a lot, Teresa, the night teller, is very understanding when she calls me up to tactfully call my attention to an error.

My *personal banker* Steve Liu helped me to get a merchant card service activated very quickly, in time for a conference at which I was giving a speech and had many potential sales for my publications. With your business account, you can investigate and take advantage of many other services that your banking institution offers. Shop around and get to know who your local community bankers are. Remember, if you've already joined your chamber of commerce, most likely you will find that they are already members too.

A competent and involved *tax planner*, who is also a Certified Public Accountant and has your best interests in mind, is another one of the people you need in your camp. For business novices, this is the person who can do more for you than just make your annual reports to the IRS look good. Accountants and attorneys are generally not good to ask for advice as they are trained to look for problems, not find you solutions. A tax planner, on the other hand is worth his or her fee if the taxes you owe both the U.S. and state governments can be lowered considerably. After all, you don't want to pay more than you have to, do you?

Learn who the movers and shakers of your community are. This is not difficult to do if you subscribe to your local or community newspaper and keep an eye on the personalities who are making the news and are featured in various articles. More likely than not, these men and women you will find to be members of the civic organizations, such as Rotary, Lions, Kiwanis, and the Soroptimists. Every one of these outstanding groups handpick their members and they are usually those who have been recognized in the business community for their leadership and community involvement. It is a golden opportunity to network with the best.

Rotary, for example, was founded over 90 years ago by a businessman named Paul Harris, who was lonely and decided to invite a few of his cronies over for group fellowship. The weekly meetings were held in turn, rotating in location from one member's home to another, thus the name Rotary. Today, Rotary International members number over 1.2 million strong, belonging to 28,134 Clubs in 518 Districts covering 154 countries worldwide.

An invaluable bonus of being a Rotarian, or member of any other civic organization among the thousands operating nationwide and globally, is that you will be immediately plugged into its extensive network. You may not think much of this aspect as you are starting up your business, but as you grow and expand both nationally and internationally, your membership will prove to be an incredible asset.

Consider this: you go on your first business trip to any city in the country and know absolutely nobody there. As a Rotarian, you would consult the Rotary International annual directory before your departure and refer to your destination, as well as the days, times, and locations of the local Rotary meetings. Schedule your travels to accommodate attendance at these locations if possible.

When you arrive at where the event is taking place, you will automatically be welcomed and have an opportunity to meet other Rotarians with whom you will make a point of exchanging your business cards. This will serve a major purpose. You will now know at least a few people in that town or city other than your business associate, customer, or client on whom you could call should you return. These local folks will be a treasure trove of information about everything from the business climate to the locations of the best places to take your client to dinner. Heck, you may even find a new golf buddy or even a potential business client.

As your business expands globally, this networking is critical. If I were to investigate doing business in Taiwan, London, or Sydney, researching and attending the meetings would be exactly where I would start. In most countries of the world, there is no such thing as cold calling. In Asia, you will not even be able to get your foot into the door of any business unless it is through an introduction or referral.

Moreover, in Asia, as in many other places around the globe, organizations such as Rotary International are elite, exclusive, and expensive. What this means is that more likely than not, only the rich and famous in the business community are invited to become members so you will be rubbing elbows with the creme de la creme of the business and industrial strata. Make no mistake about the importance of this association; you have the opportunity to immediately become connected to the top circles wherever you go.

As a novice businessperson, you may cringe at shelling out the membership fees for your local chamber or civic organization, but take my word for it, every penny is well worth being able to expand your contacts, an essential aspect of growing your business through networking.

The third membership you should seek is that in an association related to your business. In the library and online are two publications that should be a part of your required business reading right away. One is that which lists all the organizations and associations by subject matter; the second is one that provides a calendar and other pertinent information about every convention and conference that is taking place in the United States during the current year.

Once again, the networking opportunities are fantastic and you should take advantage of them. Make a point of attending at least one of these meetings or events annually and to improve your mind continuing education, uplift your spirit by surrounding yourself with those with like minds, and expand your contacts.

"No man is an island," John Donne declared, and in business, you may be surrounded by sharks, but at least you will have company.

SECRET NUMBER 5

Commitment

**Whenever you see a successful business,
someone once made a courageous
decision.**
-Peter Drucker

As a swimmer, it is only prudent to test the water before entering. So it is with your business. A home-based business is a great way to put your toe in the water before jumping in. Starting part time practically guarantees your success. Statistically, 95 percent of all businesses that originate in homes succeed during their first years. Three years later, 85 percent of them are still chugging along, compared to the 20 percent of small business that were non-home-based start-ups.

You have a lot of company because 14 million home businesses in the United States are full time and over 13.1 million are part time. Each year 500,000 new full time and 600,000 part time business startups take place. Women account for 66 percent of home business ownership for a variety of reasons such as financial need, a desire to be home with their children, divorce, no marketable skills, saving for retirement, college, and emergencies. Their earnings from home range from $6,000 to over $100,000. The top 20 percent of home-based businesses earn over $75,000 annually.

California leads the nation in the number of female-owned businesses, totaling 1.08 million companies with 2.34 million employees. Texas and New York come in next with about a half million each, followed by Florida, Illinois, Ohio, Pennsylvania, Michigan, New Jersey, and Georgia.

Minorities and new immigrants also comprise the ranks of entrepreneurs. Many have hit the glass ceilings in their companies and became discouraged and frustrated with their inability to advance to the ranks of upper management. Others may be displaced workers. From my own personal experience as both a woman and a member of a minority, I can attest that this declaration of independence boosted my feelings of self-esteem, confidence, freedom, and empowerment.

You can save a bundle on your taxes by basing your business out of your home. The square footage that you use primarily for your home office or work area, including an attached bathroom and the garage, and your utility bills are tax deductible. Find out the ins and outs of these tax breaks from your tax planner and remember to comply with your local zoning laws regulating home-based businesses. There are many restrictions regarding things like noise, increased traffic, parking, pollution, waste removal, etc. that may limit the type of business you can operate in residential neighborhoods. For example, there are big differences between providing a pet grooming or tax preparation service and doing auto tune-up or body work from your home or garage.

If you fail to plan, you plan to fail. The best theories will not succeed without a plan of action. There is much to be said about cutting your losses early in the game if you find that things are not successful. Don't let pride or stubbornness bankrupt you or your life. It is imperative that you start small and grow. Don't be too eager to quit your regular job. Remember, it is advised that you put away *at least* six months to a year's income in preparation for your business start-up. One of the gravest mistakes that an entrepreneur can make is to go out and spend a lot of money on an office, fancy furniture, and the latest equipment before the business even gets off the ground.

Even with enthusiasm, market research, a well-thought-out business plan and thorough feasibility study, operating capital, and a sure-fire idea, success is not guaranteed. Here is how I was able to test the feasibility of an idea I had before I leaped in. It was an important and valuable lesson for me and my family, but in the long run, the experience was worthwhile in many ways. Perhaps you can learn from it too.

One of my hobbies is feeding wild birds in my backyard. Because of a love of animals and nature, I thought that many others in my community also shared this activity and perhaps there was a business opportunity for a business which featured backyard birding seed delivery, supplies and gifts.

I also envisioned this concept evolving into something more: a retail business that featured "thoughtful gifts for active seniors." Having been brought up in the Chinese tradition, I respected and enjoyed being around older people. I would start with the original idea related to birdfeeding, and move toward a slightly different direction.

Norman and I also considered that it might be a good little family business that could involve our children. This concept became more and more attractive as we discussed it further. Family discussions ensued and our children agreed to become involved. Somewhere in the rosy picture, I envisioned my leaving my job at the school district, investing in and operating a store during the day, joined by and assisted by them after school.

I started doing my homework and almost everything I found out supported the idea. Statistics from a number of reliable sources indicated that feeding wild birds was extremely popular on the East Coast. It was spreading like wildfire to the West where like-minded hobbyists could engage in this activity almost year round due to the moderate climate.

"Wild bird merchandise flies at retail," declared a recent headline in the Merchandising and Marketing section of National Home Center News. "Sales of wild bird products take off," announced the magazine, citing that annual sales by people aged 16 and older of bird food and feeders exceeded $2.5 billion. It was engaged in mainly by affluent, well-educated, older Caucasians, primarily females—a demographic that well fit the community in which I lived and worked.

The growing popularity of home gardening, concern for the environment, and cross-generational interests contributed to the growing number of nature-themed stores and wild bird franchises established nationwide. One franchise grew from one store to 203 nationwide in just twelve years. Hardware and do-it-yourself home improvement stores were reporting booming sales in birdfeeding supplies and accessories.

As I continued my research, I grew more and more excited about the idea as I diligently collected statistics and copies of articles about how to market and sell to older, Depression-era, Eisenhower, and wealthy Americans, children, and by word of mouth. In my gut, I felt that everything about the concept was right, but blessed with the wisdom of maturity, experience, and age, I tempered my impulsive enthusiasm even as I was becoming obsessed with it. I planned and plotted and lost sleep in my enthusiasm, excitement, and anxiety.

Up to this point, I had spent a lot of time, but not much money, filling several loose-leaf notebooks with the information I had accumulated. My mission led me to a dozen independently-owned pet shops, large pet supply franchises, hardware and home improvement stores, and even large drugstores within a fifteen-mile radius from home. I gathered and compared detailed pricing information about various types of bird seeds and feeders. Further investigation took me to seed and feed wholesalers where I found that my orders necessitated a $100 minimum and picking up as they would be so small.

One fact uncovered in my poking around was that the big pet store franchise in one of our local shopping centers, which had space that I was considering, had a unique clause in its lease agreement. It restricted its seed wholesaler from selling and delivering 50-pound bags of seed to any other like businesses within a five-mile radius. Moreover, a wild bird franchise opened in a shopping center at the base of the peninsula. A good sign, I felt, as the owner had probably invested about $60,000 for his franchise. I felt that with regard to convenience, no overhead, and mobility, I had the advantage.

I haunted the halls of the California Mart in downtown Los Angeles where gift and home decorations and accessories are showcased. There were hundreds of things to look at, order, or buy: hanging birdfeeders, stake birdfeeders, feeders made from plaster and from terra cotta, plastic and wood. They could be ordered from dozens of sources from around the world. There were crystal hummingbirds and carved wooden cardinals, chickadees, and every other recognizable feathered creature imaginable.

I studied bird books, memorized and learned the names of common Southern California birds, went on nature hikes, looked into partnerships and franchises, drooled over appealing bird-related gifts and sent away for catalogs. Black oil sunflower seed, niger seed, peanut hearts, squirrel baffles, Lexan, merchandising and booth design, and the seasons of business all became a part of my vocabulary. The more I learned, the more questions arose that had to be addressed, and the more cautious I became. But I persisted.

I drove an hour alone to Anaheim Hills to look at Wild Birds Unlimited. Morro Bay and Santa Cruz, four and six hours away by automobile respectively, became a part of our summer vacation itinerary as these towns were among the few in which independently-owned wild bird feeding stores were. I talked to store owners, managers, and clerks, as well as to dozens of retailers and local businesspeople, and then went scouting for available retail properties all over the Palos Verdes peninsula.

Most spaces I dismissed as being too large, inconvenient, or inappropriate. About three miles away from our home, someone had built a small kiosk in a parking lot. It was located on one of the few main thoroughfares coming in and going out of the peninsula. Through the years I had passed it almost daily, and it had been used to sell hosiery, as a photo drop-off, an expresso and coffee bar, and lastly, a flower stand. I made the call and discovered that the owner wasn't interested in leasing or renting it out.

Another possibility was a free-standing little cottage at a major intersection next to and across the street from a group of real estate offices. Further investigation revealed that the city of Rolling Hills had limited its use to services only and a retail business was not permitted at that location.

A successful comic book store had moved to larger quarters on one of the major streets in our community and I coveted both its size and location. At night I would sit in my parked car in the parking lot across the street, gazing at its darkened, empty windows and mentally designing its interior. It was a half a block away from the one and only post office in the community and opposite an open mall that boasted one of two major drugstores in the area, a successful gourmet food market and bakery, and a whole row of other stores.

But I also recognized the downside of the place too. It had a cracked and bulging sidewalk out front, its existing signage was inadequately lit and not sufficiently visible from the street, not accessible to physically-challenged, wheelchair-bound, elderly customers, or more importantly, for the delivery of pallets of 50-pound bags of birdseed out front or back.

Finally, after almost nine months of research, planning, analysis and preparation, we were ready to test both the idea and the market. Brainstorming with a number of friends, we settled on the name of Wild Wings 'n Things. We limited ourselves to a budget of several thousand dollars and reserved a 10' x 10' booth at an upcoming two-day, local wine and food festival, and our foray into retailing was launched. I justified the rather steep $1500 booth fee with the thought that it was the first of similar community events leading up to the holidays and I could catch the gift-giving public. (For a point of reference, most street fair booths range between $50 to $350 and that fee alone could pay for two weeks of booth space at the Los Angeles County Fair.)

From the onset, our business was meant to be an experiment and we put a limit on our budget, promising ourselves that we would re-evaluate the trial after three, six, and nine months. It was critical to my family and me to test the market before we committed ourselves to a three-year lease on retail store space and tens of thousands of dollars to stocking the store with merchandise. We knew the market would expect and respond to a well-designed booth that would showcase the birding supplies and gifts, so Norman and I spent hours at Pasadena's Fall Arts and Crafts Fair which featured over three hundred booths. We observed, evaluated, and argued the merits and weaknesses of various booth styles and construction. Then, a week before Wild Wings 'n Things was to debut, he and our son Steven spent a weekend designing and creating cedar lattice modules for the booth's walls. The cost in materials alone was over $500.

Next came the task of stocking the booth. Although foreign-made gift items were cheaper, they did not meet the high standards of quality and the "look" I wanted. I soon discovered that many American manufacturers of gift items required minimum orders of $200 to $250 for their goods, so I had to carefully pick and choose the merchandise that I wanted to carry in the booth. There were shipping and freighting charges to pay from suppliers all over the United States, and no guarantees of refunds or replacements for damaged goods delivered, nor of arrival dates. To add variety and to save money, a few items were purchased singly and at retail prices.

When I reached my budget limit, we assembled the entire booth in our driveway, from the walls to the display tables to the lighting and everything that would be on sale. The impression I got was that it was sparse and my mom and dad encouraged me to purchase more items to fill out the booth, so I added merchandise. Books, craft sets, birdfeeders, seed, seasonal baskets and accessories, seed scoops, and at the very last minute, decorative house banners distributed by a friend and neighbor were added to the wares in the Wild Wings 'n Things booth.

Publicizing the business wasn't difficult for me as I generated a catchy media release and supplied my photograph, both of which were published in the local newspaper. As a director of the chamber of commerce, I was able to arrange for a genuine ribbon-cutting with the president and other directors. Friends and family were informed by both word of mouth and invitation and the big day arrived.

That first event was a learning experience, just as every other decision and move relating to Wild Wings 'n Things has been ever since. In two subsequent street fairs and six Sundays at the local farmers' market following, we learned to simplify everything. Although our first booth took *six* hours to set up, by December it was up and running in forty-five minutes. Bulky, heavy, six-foot-long, folding utility tables were replaced by light, wooden boards resting on collapsible pipe legs purchased from a swap meet supplier. We also bought clamps, bungee straps, and a dining canopy from a sporting goods store for $85, deciding not to invest in a $200 telescoping vinyl canopy from a local grocery warehouse.

We acquired new respect for those hardy souls who made a living exhibiting at swap meets, and for those artisans whose crafts took them from fair to fair every weekend, travelling all over the state and country. We learned that business success was not a straight path, and could take us in new, unforeseen directions. The decorative house banners, poles, and brackets were our best-sellers, keeping the rest of the business afloat. My spare hours were spent poring over books on sales strategies and listening to audio tapes on the psychology of selling in my car. On many nights, I could be found wielding my glue gun with glee as I crafted holiday baskets in our unheated garage.

I learned first and foremost, that you are never fully compensated for all the time you put into your business start-up ,because we did not factor in how much of our time was dedicated to Wild Wings 'n Things. As the year drew to a close, the novelty of the business began to wear thin and the interest and involvement of our teenagers dwindled. But they gamely continued to join me later on Sundays to help pack up, even as I got up early and alone on Sunday mornings to set up the booth by myself. I wanted to give the project a chance at least through the holiday season, and then we would re-evaluate.

There was no end to the education we all got from starting and running Wild Wings 'n Things. We were encouraged and proud at the compliments about our merchandise and booth design. The most common remark we heard were, "What an adorable booth," and "You have a lot of cute/nice things here." People asked if we had a store and we answered them honestly, that we were testing the market to determine whether we should open one.

We found that in September Californians had not begun to think about holiday decorations or gift-giving, that people buy from those who they like, and good eye contact, a friendly smile and taking time with customers could generate sales. That consumers and the markets, even a niche such as ours, are unpredictable, just as my wise friend and experienced gift retailer Marylyn Ginsburg told me. That you can never absolutely or accurately predict or project what will sell at any time or season. That for all the billions spent on marketing research, retailing is still a crap shoot. That if it weren't, all retail businesses would all be wildly successful, but they aren't.

We had fun, worked hard, made a lot of friends and some money, and met many people along the way. There was the sympathetic booth owner who watched me make eight trips back and forth to unload my van and declared, "You have a lot of little things." And the African-American attorney who created and sold silk floral arrangements as her "therapy," and Steve and Bea, the couple who sold cotton clothing in the booth next to ours at craft Sundays at the local farmers' market. It was Bea who confided that although she had several stores, retailing was not all it was cut out to be. We would get more traffic, she intimated, in a four-hour period at the farmers' market on a Sunday than during an entire week at one of her shops.

Getting up early on Sunday mornings wasn't so bad. The weather was almost always beautiful, the air crisp and clean, and chatting with and selling to the community was a lot of fun. It gave me a chance to experience in small measure, what owning and operating a family retail business with and without assistance of all its members would be like.

The most important lesson we learned was that a retail business was not for us and there were just too many other things competing for our family's time and attention, both individually and as a unit. The resources we expended on Wild Wings 'n Things was our tuition. We did not think of one minute or one penny of it as being wasted, for it was worth finding out the truth about ourselves and the potential of the business. We gave it our best effort and at least made some profit but we all agreed that testing the water first saved us from getting in over our heads in the long run. Thus we were able to save ourselves from making a major mistake that might have cost us tens or hundreds of thousands of dollars.

Do you have an idea for a new or improved product? About twenty years ago, my husband did. He would habitually make two tears from the edges of the plastic covers of the cups of coffee he bought. This he did so that he could sip the liquid without spilling. Every time I saw him do that, I always remarked that I thought it a clever solution to prevent spilling.

"How about going into business making a cover that is already scored for other coffee drinkers?" I suggested. We had a great idea but never acted on it. Today we are reminded of it each time we purchase a cup of coffee or soda with a premoulded plastic cover that prevents spills. The first covers were simple; but in the tradition of "building a better mousetrap," or in this case, a cup cover, the designs have become pretty fancy. These second and third generation improved versions sport little "buttons" to push down to indicate whether the liquid within is black coffee, has cream or sugar, or identifies the type of soda inside.

A new product involves the greatest risk. Thousands of things are introduced into the market annually, costing approximately $20 million each to launch. Only a few become winners. Those which make their inventors and creators rich and famous are ones, just like the cup cover that prevents spills and yet permits drinking, that meet a consumer need. They cause people to say, "What a great idea!"

But getting a positive response when you show or tell your friends and family is just the beginning, but barely enough on which to stake your future and fortune. Just as the three most important keys to success in real estate are location, location, location, launching a new product or idea requires testing, testing, testing.

You need to show your idea or a drawing or prototype to at least a dozen people to get their candid, initial reaction. You must ask questions consistently, such as:

- How much would you pay for this? (perceived value)
- How often would you use it? (market)
- How often would you buy this? (projected sales)
- Where would you find such a product? (outlets/distributors)
- Would you invest in this product? (the true test!)

You've got a lot of homework to do (review **Secret Number 4**), and even then, there's no guarantee of great success, just as we discovered with Wild Wings 'n Things. You will need to research associations and organizations as well as sales data for similar products. Find out what the standard mark-up is for such items, what the national sales figures were for the past few years and what the projected sales will be in the next year, as well as three and five years ahead.

Our experience proved how important a feasibility study is to a business start-up. Prepare your marketing plan, raise money, create prototypes to be placed into retail stores and businesses. What *kind* of distribution channels will you employ? What *types* of stores will carry your product? There are specialty, discount, department, outlets, you name it, we've got 'em all over the country.

Research, research, research. Test, test, test.

Magazines such as *INC.*, *Entrepreneur,* and *SUCCESS* should be on your regular reading list for they and similar publications are devoted to entrepreneurs. These will provide you with the latest news, trends, and information. Just remember to keep your day job and don't hock your house and your possessions quite yet.

Good luck. You're going to need lots!

Lifting Off

LESSON NUMBER 6
Faith

**Full throttle ahead. Hold back a little
and you'll never get off the ground.**
-Flying instructor

There comes a time when you must take the first step on your thousand-mile journey. You have prepared in every way you can—planned, schemed, analyzed, made projections and created a business plan, arranged for everything from financing to renting your post office box and postage meter machine. Your business cards and letterhead stationery have been delivered and a business account has been opened at your local bank. The time has arrived when you must now launch your business.

Did the feeling come on suddenly, or did it creep up on you? You find yourself hesitating just a tad. Doubts about this whole entrepreneur thing begin to insinuate themselves in your mind. Now you're experiencing a bit of anxiety, lose a bit of your confidence, and begin wondering if this entire business startup wasn't a big mistake after all. "Courage is doing what you're afraid to do," Eddie Rickenbacker told us; "there can be no courage unless you're scared."

Everything you have done up to this point was like preparing the soil for planting your seeds of success. You are now poised like the airline pilot preparing for his flight. He walks around and inspects his aircraft, climbs on aboard, checks his dials and instruments, and revs up the engines before he taxis to the head of the runway. And after getting the go-ahead from the control tower, he pulls the throttle back all the way, giving the aircraft the necessary surge of power to accelerate down the runway until it reaches the speed at which it can lift off. If the throttle isn't engaged 100 percent, the plane will never get off the ground. So it is with your business.

Franklin D. Roosevelt recognized the debilitating power of fear. One of the most quoted lines from his first inaugural speech delivered on March 4, 1933, is, "Let me assert my firm belief that the only thing we have to fear is fear itself." As a longtime volunteer trainer and mentor to entrepreneurs in training for the National Association of Women Business Owners, the American Women's Economic Development Council, and the Academy of Business Leadership at the University of Southern California, I am always struck by the comments shared by the participants.

"It's scary," is the most common one. Yes, I acknowledge, it is scary, because you are venturing into the unknown and taking risks. It is safer and far more secure to stay where you are now, just as a ship in the harbor is safe. But that's not what ships are for.

Have confidence in all the time and effort, research and planning you have invested up to now. Throw back your shoulders and close your eyes, envisioning and affirming yourself and your abilities. Mentally say, "I can do it. I *am* doing it. I'm off!" Take several full, deep, slow breaths, open your eyes and focus them on your goal at the end of the runway and pull back on the throttle all the way to send your endeavor into motion.

"Before everything else, getting ready is the secret of success," said Henry Ford. Do not hesitate nor allow any negative thoughts encroach upon your heart or mind. Don't hold back, not even a little bit. Your business, whatever it is and just like an aircraft, cannot lift off if you haven't given it full throttle, full power—*100 percent.* Once you have taken that first step, you must stay concentrated on your tasks to get yourself off the ground. If you believe it, you will achieve it. It's that simple, and it *is* all in your head.

This is the most crucial time for your start up. *Nothing* should break your concentration on getting your project up to the proper elevation for coasting. Your attitude will determine your altitude.

Do you think attitude doesn't make a difference? You bet it does! Try this very important experiment with a friend or family member and see for yourself.

Stand and lift up one of your arms until it is straight out from your shoulders. Instruct the other person to wrap two hands around any part of that arm and to pull it down when you give a nod of your head.

Close your eyes, lift up your chin, and in your head, think the very best thing about yourself: I am a fantastic cook. I play a great game of golf (or tennis, or whatever sport you excel in). I am a good father (or mother) to my children. I am a very honest, law-abiding citizen. I am an excellent_____, well, you fill in the blank. Whatever you choose to think about yourself, it must be a positive affirmation of you as a person, or of your unique skills.

Nod your head and see what happens. Your companion will have great difficulty in pulling your arm down, whatever his or her size or strength.

Now give the same instructions to that person. In this second experiment, you are going to think the very worst thing about yourself. I yelled at my son, daughter, spouse, or employee today. I am a terrible parent. I am a lousy _____(you name it.) I can't swim, sing, play the piano, or whatever, worth a damn. Nod your head a second time. The result will be entirely different.

These two activities illustrate the greatest power in the world—that of your mind. Knowing how to use that power is one of your secrets to entrepreneurship. Squelch every hesitation, anxiety, and negative thought right now and proceed as if you cannot fail.

SECRET NUMBER 7

Empowerment

**There is only one success—
to be able to spend your life
in your own way.**
-Christopher Morley

A
s your business becomes established, you will hear many definitions of success. Success is getting what you want. Happiness is wanting what you get. "If people knew what they had to do to be successful, most people wouldn't," said Lord Thomson of Fleet. "The toughest thing about success is that you've got to keep on being a success," Irving Berlin, is quoted. Cindy Adams told us that success has made failures of many men, and Oscar Wilde claimed that: Success is a science. If you have the conditions, you get the results. All of these are probably true for somebody, maybe for you.

Success is *whatever* you define it as being, *whatever* you perceive it to be, *wherever* you want it to be, *whenever* you want it to be. Do not let anybody else determine or articulate it for you, for only you know what it means to you. It could be for richer or poorer, sooner or later. If being fabulously wealthy is your idea of success, that it is. If being a celebrity and guest on every currently popular talk show is your idea of success, that's okay too. Nobody but you can recognize it better than you.

Songwriter Harry Chapin's father described it thus: "Success in pursuit of other people's dreams leaves you feeling a bad kind of tired, while even failure in pursuit of your own dreams leaves you with an exhausted satisfaction."

But you will have achieved it at the very moment, day, or occasion when you can unequivocally declare, "I've done it. *This is it.*" At that very instant, you will have validated every effort you have made, every penny you have invested, every moment you have spent on establishing your business. It is the moment at which the plane has reached its cruising altitude and speed. However, until then, you cannot withhold your enthusiasm or restrict your momentum.

Very often your success is measured in very small increments. Make a point of being optimistic and cheerful as you go about your tasks each day. Be joyous in all the things that you do. If you keep your face to the sunshine, you will never see the shadows. Nor will you allow them to encroach upon the light in your life. Accentuating the positive, like the old song advises, is a smart attitude to take. Research has proven that physically, you can avoid head and backaches, heart disease, and digestive ailments. If you stay upbeat, you will be energized as you go about your day and your business.

Be grateful for the little, good things that happen to you daily. They are the squares that make up the tapestry of your days and your life. It only takes one day during which everything goes wrong for you to value all the things and days that go right. Finding a parking space, missing a traffic jam, the smooth hum that indicates that your faxed document was sent without getting mangled in the machine, arriving at a business appointment or picking up your child from school on time, the crazy driver who missed you when he swerved his car...these are the good things to appreciate and be grateful for. A lot of things can get on your nerves, but only if you *let* them.

Thank whichever higher power you believe in for the minutiae, the simple, yet important things which occurred smoothly each day. Don't ever take them for granted. When you think of all the things that could go wrong, but didn't, you have a lot to be thankful for every day. Keep your perspective about situations by discriminating between what is a real emergency and what is not. You know what I mean. Your getting a flat tire pales in comparison to your son getting arrested by the police for shoplifting.

Maintaining your equilibrium is a habit you need to develop early as you embark on your journey, just like the steady, firm hands of the pilot that guide the plane as it soars into the sky. You have control over how much time you will devote to your family and to your business; set aside for yourself and the people who you cherish around you. It's not easy to work out of your home because everything that is comfortable for you is also nearby to distract you: the children, bills, kitchen, and all of the details associated with your personal life.

It takes a lot of willpower to set aside specific hours during which you will be conducting your business from home. Mine begin after my husband and children have left for work and school. One thing I've learned over the years was to be there with and for the rest of the family in the morning until the last one was out the door. No business calls could be answered or made until I was alone in the house. Okay, okay. I do confess to sneaking in telephone calls to the East Coast before 7 a.m. to save money on long-distance charges while my hubby was in the shower.

In the afternoon, things get a lot fuzzier. The children returning from school at around 3:30 p.m. require my attention and it happens also to be during the last two and half hours of the business day. And then, if you're the designated cook as well, you will soon find it is time to begin preparing dinner for your family. You need to work out a daily schedule that is the most comfortable for everyone concerned, and try your best to stick to it.

Keep in mind the eloquence of Reinhold Niebuhr, author of the Serenity Prayer :

O God, give us serenity to accept what cannot be
changed; courage to change what should be changed,
and wisdom to distinguish the one from the other.

Convince yourself and *believe* that most things in life are those that you can not change, have control over, or have responsibility for. You don't have control over, nor are you responsible for the traffic, weather, government, world and local economies, other people, their moods, feelings, or their lives, and just about everything else in the universe. If you suddenly get caught in a bumper-to-bumper snarl, there's no need to become angry or frustrated. Tell yourself that it was not in your power to do anything about it. Do not blame anybody or anything. Turn on your radio to your favorite station or load up your favorite CD or an inspirational tape, take some deep breaths to relax and relieve your tension. Just be sure to do the professional thing and either get off the highway to call or dial your cellular phone to apologize as well as inform your client that you will be late.

While you do not have control over time, you can control what you do with yours. Don't go around complaining that you don't have time to do this or that. Everyone in the world has exactly twenty-four hours in a day, no more or no less. Thomas Edison, Leonardo da Vinci, William Shakespeare, John Glenn, and Martin Luther King had only twenty-four in theirs. So did Madame Curie, Mother Teresa, Stephen Hawkins, Jackie Joyner-Kirsee, Michael Chang, Michael Johnson, Michael Jackson, and Michael Jordan. Whoever you name, dead or alive, is given that same gift.

The Chinese say: The emperor is rich, but he cannot buy one extra year. The greatest difference in our lives are the choices we make as to *how* we use that gift of each new day. Knowing how to manage your time is one of the greatest skills that you as an entrepreneur should possess. Many of them I know get up earlier to get their work done *before* the phones start ringing and the interruptions begin. Best-selling author John Grisham worked on his book *A Time to Kill* every morning beginning at 5 a.m. for three years. My daughter Jamie's friend, Olympic gold medalist Michelle Kwan and her dad, rose at 4 a.m. daily to make the two-hour drive from Torrance to Lake Arrowhead for her daily skating practice. The first draft of this book was mostly written on a laptop computer during business air flights.

It's up to you to make the time to accomplish your dreams and goals. Listen to your body and follow its natural rhythms. If you are a morning person, get up earlier; if you're a night owl, stay up later. Whichever you choose, do get enough rest. If you suffer from sleep deprivation, you will be of no use to anyone or anything, including the business you've worked so hard to build.

Time doesn't really exist, except as an abstract concept in your head. The present moment is the only time you have. Make something of this moment! Mark Twain once remarked that he had been through some terrible things in his life, some of which actually happened! Isn't this so true? Somewhere I heard that 80 percent of what you worry about never happens. Deal with the 20 percent as life dishes it out, one moment at a time. Our tendency can be to put ourselves through hell in our mind, contemplating and worrying about what could come to pass. Yet, if we look at the present moment, which is all we have, there is no great problem at all! Live it in the now and savor it.

Don't waste your time doing things you don't want or like to do. This was one of my resolutions that I made during my recovery from cancer. After all, you became an entrepreneur to enjoy your life more, remember? Even years ago, when I turned thirty years old, I had already begun practicing this.

I made a conscious decision not to let my life take over my *living*. I become very protective of which organizations I donated too, which meetings I attended, who I spent my lunch or dinner time with, and so on. "Learn to say no," Charles Haddon Spurgeon counseled, "it will be of more use to you than to be able to read Latin." This may be difficult to do but imperative to free you to be more productive and effective as an entrepreneur.

I myself choose very carefully and limit myself to just a few favorite organizations. When you take on anything new, be sure to let something else go. For example, when I joined Rotary,

I resigned as a director on the board of the local chamber of commerce, but remained an active member. To all other requests to join or serve you can say, "I am honored that your organization has considered me for its board (this position, etc.) but I can only commit if I can do it well because I don't want to let you or the organization down. If I cannot do it to the best of my ability, it is a matter of personal integrity that I decline this invitation at this time. Please understand that it is not due to lack of interest in or support for your cause, but rather to limits of my time and energy. If you have another way I can be of assistance to your group, please call me."

The ability to say no does not mean that you have abandoned your community, but rather empowers you to pick and choose specific activities for which you have the interest, time and energy. Many of these require just a few hours and not that you regularly attend meetings. My volunteer work, for example, still includes being a docent for historical walking tours of Los Angeles Chinatown, conducting lectures and seminars to a range of audiences on a myriad of topics, mentoring students and entrepreneurs, writing for several publications, and presenting at numerous school, professional and civic groups. If I can't give my time, I make a donation of money or services.

Acknowledge that you are not superhuman and be particular about to whom and what you give your valuable time and stamina. What activities could you be a part of that would fit your schedule and lifestyle? Consider yourself honored when you are asked to be a speaker at any event because it is a clear indication that someone has noticed you and is convinced that you have something to share to an audience. Accept such invitations and other requests for your time and talent. Just don't bite off more than you can chew. Choose how much or how little you want to be involved, but do volunteer for at least one thing.

I work hard so that I can afford to pay other people to do the things that I am unable to do. My time is precious and I *choose* not to spend it, for example, cooking elaborate Chinese gourmet meals for my family who prefer simpler fare anyway. It is worth my peace of mind to give certain chores to someone else. You too, have better things to do with your life, right? Like conquering the business world as an entrepreneur. As Mary Kay Ash of Mary Kay Cosmetics puts it so well: "Don't waste dollar time on penny jobs."

We are all guilty of falling into this trap. You tell yourself, "I'll do it myself because it will cost a lot of money to pay somebody else to." And because you are so busy, the task doesn't get done. Meanwhile you lose the use of that piece of equipment or whatever it is, until finally, a crises develops and you end up paying someone else to do it anyway, sometimes even more because you need it in a hurry. Don't be penny wise and pound foolish. The old adage has a lot of truth: You do have to spend money to make money. Just be sure to spend it (and your time) in the right places, most importantly to your effectiveness as an owner and manager of your own business in order to liberate yourself from tasks that you could delegate to others.

Think of how many times you may have experienced this exact scenario in your personal life or know of someone who has. The lesson learned is to concentrate only on those activities that will have payback for you and your business. Let go of or delegate those that do not move you toward your goals and dreams. It takes hard-earned experience to make the right choices.

A speaker I heard once said, "Yesterday is history, tomorrow is a mystery. We only have today, and that's why it's call the present." "Do what you can, with what you have, where you are," Theodore Roosevelt told us. We women are always trying to fix things that go wrong. Well, men do too, but often it is unwise, inappropriate, or impossible for you to do anything about a situation. You cannot fix everything. This is where that wisdom in the Serenity Prayer makes good sense. Efficient people get things done. Effective people get the *right* things done.

Refrain from "beating" yourself up, emotionally, mentally, or physically. Take good care of your body as it's the only one you'll ever have. Take good care of your mind and it will take care of you. Don't waste your todays or tomorrows by worrying about the yesterdays. Let go, let go, *LET GO*!

Make your hands into tight fists and hold them out to your sides. Many of us are like those fists, closed or grasping on so tightly to old habits, stereotypes, prejudices, opinions, paradigms, methods, or philosophies. Closed hands also represent closed minds and hearts that are non-productive and non-creative.

Now open up those fists wide. What do you see? Turn your head from side to side and take a good, hard look at your open palms. They represent openness that can attract all sorts of things—opportunities and butterflies, ideas and new life. Wiggle your fingers and move them around. They could be molding a priceless sculpture, directing an orchestra, holding a tennis racket or the golf club in a championship game, typing on computer keys that unlock the mysteries of technology. What are your hands doing? Are they open? Remember that you cannot grab for the gusto in life if your hands are closed into fists.

By insisting on keeping balance in your life, you will live long and live well. After all, what's the point of your living to a ripe old age if the quality of that life is lousy?

To illustrate this critical point, cut a length of string or yarn about a foot in length. Arrange it twice: once in a gently, wavy line; the second time, in sharp, vertical peaks and valleys. Notice that the width of your project is longer in the first instance and much shorter in the second. The yarn remains the same length, but it is how it was arranged that made the difference in its length. Your life is like that piece of string. You can shorten or lengthen it by living it purposefully and gently with natural, little ups and downs. Or you can contribute to shortening your time on earth by allowing everything and everyone around you take over. Once again, it is your choice, and yours alone.

At the beginning of last year, I decided to slow down and take things easier than I had been doing since I founded my business almost eight years ago. No sooner had I made that decision, all sorts of business and opportunities opened up to me. To make a long story short, I made 29 business trips in ten months, some to cities such as Las Vegas, San Francisco, Portland, and Seattle, two, three, or four times. Other travels took me to cities to which I had never or rarely been to before: Chicago, St. Louis, Denver, Atlanta, Cleveland, Boston, Houston, and Brownsville.

Years ago, when my husband was an employee of Hughes Aircraft Company, he did a lot of business travelling. Stuck at home with four young children, I was extremely envious of him whose itineraries would include places like Paris, Tokyo, Toronto, and Washington, D.C.

"It gets tiresome and the novelty wears out soon," he told me but I was not convinced. Years later, as I began to travel alone on my business trips, I realized the truth of his words. Shlepping through long airport terminals, pulling a wheeled suitcase, with the strap of my laptop computer bag biting into my shoulder, at times I've felt like a pack horse! Curbside check-in of heavier luggage *before* I return the rental car now saves my back and allows me to board unencumbered.

In whichever city or hotel I was, I was eating and sleeping alone. Being with my clients during the daytime hours and not returning to my accommodations until after dark, there weren't too many places I could hang out and relax. It's not easy for a woman alone to go down to the hotel bar, order a drink, and watch the Monday Night Football with a group of strangers.

But experience is a wonderful teacher. Just in the past ten months, I have made 28 trips and have now learned to pack easily, lightly and well, almost to the point of Spartan.. I don't carry more than I need. Even a hairdryer weighing just a few pounds is borrowed from the hotel, rather than added to my luggage. Expensive or favorite jewelry and clothing are best left at home. You don't want to attract unwanted attention in public places nor have them lost, stolen, or accidentally left behind.

The best habit I've learned is to arrive at my business destination a day early. Driving my rental car from the airport to the hotel, I get a good sense of the traffic so I know how to drive in it. (My Uncle Benny takes this a step further and even makes a dry run from his hotel to the location of his appointment a day early to familiarize himself with the route.) I take note of landmarks along the way, go shopping, enjoy local tourist attractions, and treat myself to dinner.

This routine prepares me for my next day, usually spent conducting my business, and yet the trip has not disintegrated into a slam-bang event which is rough on my body and my mind. Rather, it creates a mini-vacation during which I do things I enjoy while I am travelling. I get to see the country, experiencing the culture and the people in various cities from coast to coast. For those of you who work at home, it can be a luxury that becomes a necessity in order to balance your life. Most importantly, I've created precious time for myself in a stimulating, new environment, something that's difficult to do when working from home. Those extra dollars I've spent are an investment in my physical and mental health, and much more fun than going to a therapist or experiencing crushing stress.

The ability to pace yourself is one you need to develop in your life. Take those business trips that I just mentioned, for example. Plan your itinerary, purchase your ticket, reserve your accommodations and rental car in advance. Pack clothing that you can coordinate as well as wear in layers according to the weather at your destination. (Recently I was told that the low was 30 degrees and the high was in the 50s for an upcoming January trip to Houston. I arrived to eighty-degree temperatures and sunny, cloudless days, but I had the foresight to include lighter clothing with my woolen sweaters.) Allow yourself plenty of time to travel to the airport, park your car, check your luggage, go through security, and arrive at the departure gate in time for your flight.

At your destination, read the local newspapers, watch the city's news on television at night, chat with the shopkeepers and hotel personnel, arrange for a wake-up call in the morning, and go to bed at a decent time. If you see something you wish to purchase while you're out of town, indulge yourself and get it, or you may find yourself either wasting time later trying to get back to the store or having regrets at not doing so later. Remember that two major benefits of entrepreneurship are liberation and empowerment. You can spend your hard-earned money, *guilt-free*, on whatever and whomever you like.

Don't forget to bring an extra pair of glasses, sunglasses, contact lenses, or the prescription for eyewear you use, any medication you take, your driver's license, auto and health insurance cards, a small shoe sponge, a clothes or safety pin or two (to keep hotel drapes closed and the room dark), breath mints, frequent flyer and long-distance phone cards, and several ziplock plastic bags. Keep a supply of raisins, trail mix, or protein bars in your carry-on or briefcase, or purchase fresh fruit to keep in the car. You'll never know when and where your next meal might occur.

It's a good idea to keep in mind Murphy's Law: everything that can go wrong, will. There are too many things beyond your control, especially when you travel on business. You will never know what the traffic's going to be like on the way to the airport or how long it will take for you to drive around to find a parking space. You may go to the wrong terminal or encounter a long, unanticipated walk to the departure gate for your connection. Your flight may have been cancelled or there may be five men in front of you at the security gate, each one having to remove the contents of his pockets before he can pass through. Worse yet, the six people ahead of you could all have laptop computers that the security staff asks to unpack and turn on.

The rental car counter may be closed because your flight was late getting in, or the shuttle to the hotel may have stopped running for the night and you need to call, then wait for the next one. It may be raining or snowing, or there may be a tornado alert or hurricane watch in effect. If you're destined for California, we might even have had an earthquake the day of your arrival, just to welcome you. Did you factor in how far away the rental cars were parked from the terminal or how long it took for the shuttle to get you from the lot to and from the airport?

Familiarize yourself with the controls of the vehicle and the route you are taking to your destination *before* you leave that rental car lot. There's nothing more nerve-wracking than getting lost on strange highways, neighborhoods, and cities to add spice to your life! Don't go cheap when you travel. The money you think you are saving is not worth losing your peace of mind if you end up in a less than safe part of town. Invest the few dollars on a rental automobile that has the Global Positioning System which will direct you electronically, visually, and by audio to every destination and appointment. This is not the time to be a tightwad because personal safety and security have their own price. Be willing to pay it.

Always bring copies of your correspondence, address, and telephone number of your client with you on your trip. Get in the habit of using a clear, concise shorthand when taking down directions and always read them, phone and fax numbers, and other information back to the person:

-L (N) Morrison Street
-6 blks
-R Clay
-Keep R
-I-105 N
-Exit 7th Street
-L @ end of ramp
-4-5 mi on R #28928 7th (415) 234-5678

Keep the hotel address with you when you go out and remember your room number. If you are using public telephones, speak clearly and softly so that others around you do not gather overhear information about your personal activities. Be wary about the people with whom you have conversations at restaurants and hotels. Ladies, double your purse strap around the hook on the restroom stall door for extra security. Wash your hands as often as you can because every surface you touch is crawling with cooties: handles, doorknobs, elevator buttons, currency and coins. Use the paper towels you wiped your hands with to open restroom doors.

Do most of your packing the night before your departure, leaving only the last-minute essentials to put away in your luggage. On check-out day, open every drawer, closet and cabinet to be certain you haven't left something behind. Check under the beds and behind the shower curtain. Eat a healthy breakfast and always leave a generous tip for the breakfast waitress and for the person who has to clean up after you at the hotel.

If you're being met by a client or limousine driver at an airport, be sure to specify the location at which you will meet. Will it be at the arrival gate, just outside the security check, down in baggage claim, or out at curbside? Don't take anything for granted. Once I waited almost an hour for the limo driver to meet me at the arrival gate. A woman saw me waiting during that time, came up to me near the end of the hour and asked, "Are you waiting for someone to pick you up?" When I answered in the affirmative, she told me that people without tickets were not permitted to enter pass the security check. Thanking her, I rushed through the terminal, and sure enough, there was a very frantic limousine driver waiting on the other side of the x-ray conveyor belt. On another occasion, the driver waited for me at the baggage claim while I was upstairs at arrivals. Consider meeting your contact at the *departure area* to avoid the crowds and delays at the baggage claim where the arriving passengers usually converge.

Smile at and thank those with whom you come in contact with: the airline personnel who waited on you on your flight, the pilots who brought you safely to your destination, the hotel staff. Treat each business trip like the adventure that it is and learn lessons along the way. Keep a travel journal. There's something to be gained each time you travel that will add to your experience: how to plan and pack more efficiently, what to bring and not to bring on your travels, which airline serves your favorite soda and the best meals, which items in your wardrobe travel the best, which travel agent can get your tickets to you on time, etc.

Be sure to include a supply of your letterhead stationery, envelopes, and stamps in a folder on your trips. During or at the end of each day, jot down what you recall about each person you meet on his or her business card, the date, event, and the city. You can begin handwriting your thank yous and notes to those from whom you have collected business cards during your journey. This will allow you to get a head start on your correspondence in flight while the details and impressions are still fresh in your mind.

SECRET NUMBER 8

marketing Yourself

**Success is not so much what you are,
but rather what you appear to be.**
-Anonymous

Years ago when I first moved to the Washington, D.C. area, I observed that many African Americans were driving expensive Lincoln and Cadillac sedans around town. I was extremely impressed that so many members of this particular ethnic group enjoyed financial success and affluent lifestyles. Even in the tiny Northwest section of the District in which we lived among diplomats and legislators, I did not see as many of these types of elegant automobiles.

Then one day I had the occasion to drive through a poor neighborhood and was shocked at the poverty that I saw. Uncollected trash and garbage lined the curbs and streets, boarded up windows and buildings were the norm, and shabbily-dressed denizens abound. But what struck me the most was that many of the automobiles parked in the streets were the same elegant models that I had seen driven by African Americans around the rest of the city.

Confused by this discovery, I asked my father why the poor people spent so much money on their cars.

"Many more people will see them in their fancy cars than in their poor homes and therefore will get the impression that they are wealthy," he explained.

We don't have a second chance to make a first impression. In every sense of the word, perception is reality. Research has shown that people show more respect towards others who are well groomed and well dressed than those who are not. The same man may enter a crowded elevator on two different occasions, impeccably dressed and scruffily dressed, and get two different reactions from those already there.

You can test this theory out yourself. Go to an upscale boutique or the fine jewelry or handbag section of a department store dressed in jeans, faded T-shirt and athletic shoes one day and in your Sunday or business best another. Notice how the salespeople speak and respond to, as well as treat you. The way they do will give you a good idea of how appearances make a tremendous difference in the way you are perceived.

Your business and the way you conduct it works the same way. Everything from how you answer the telephone to the way you, your letterhead, stationery, and office look says volumes about you. Are you and your entire staff friendly, professional, and businesslike in your manner? Is everything that you do representative of your best joint effort? Everything should be topnotch, the best you can afford, to project the best impression.

The Sicilians say that a fish stinks from the head down. There is truth to this old saying, and it applies to households as well as to businesses, large and small. You, as the head, create the culture of your company with vision, mission, imagination, passion, planning, perspective, persistence, and perspiration. The most effective and profitable companies are those in which everyone shares those same common goals. Make no mistake about it, when all have moral and emotional ownership, the organization thrives. 'Good management," John D. Rockefeller told us, "consists of showing average people how to do the work of superior people."

Step back and take an honest look at your business and ask yourself the following questions:

- Does it value cultural diversity and the individual's achievements and accomplishments?
- Does its environment encourage and support personal and professional growth?
- Does it reward its employees with appreciation for their contributions to the good health and prosperity of the company?
- Is it family-friendly?
- Are you a kind, compassionate, fair, inspirational, wise, and visionary leader?
- Are you able to acknowledge and recognize the individual and combined talent of everyone who works in the company?
- Are people happy to come to work each day?
- Is *synergy* propelling your company and its personnel forward?

As an individual, you have a unique communication and learning style. The ways you think, do, and react to things and situations are the result of your upbringing. Take stock of yourself as a leader and the way you operate. Are you a doer, thinker, intuiter, or feeler? Are you an introvert or an extrovert? What are the styles of those with whom you work and have business and social relationships? Even in a marriage, a clash of styles can cause friction, but unequivocally, the person who can relate to other people on all four levels comfortably is the most successful leader. There are many excellent books about effective communication that you can borrow from the library or purchase at your local bookstore to help you understand and become more effective as a manager of people.

In the first few seconds of an encounter with another person, you are being sized up. Ethnicity, gender, and age are the first three things that somebody will notice in the initial ten seconds of meeting you, according to Janet Larsen Palmer of the Communication Excellence Institute. In addition, within half a minute, you've been assessed according to your appearance, facial expression, eye contact, movement patterns, personal space, and touch.

Whether you are a one-man or one-woman business or a multi-national, multi-billion-dollar corporation, meeting at your local chamber's monthly mixer or videoconferencing by state-of-the-art communication satellite, that first impression still boils down to comfort level. Will you fit into the other person's world? If you are perceived as fitting in, you're on your way to relating to each other. If not, you will fail to connect and opportunities will be lost. Don't forget that in today's global community, cultural communication styles differ greatly between individuals and countries. The savvy businessperson is sensitive and aware of these differences and learns skills to minimize the differences and maximize the commonalities.

Appearances and the professional conduct of your business cements your position. Just like the impoverished owners of the luxury cars in Washington, D.C., you create the impression, both for yourself and your company. Like a wall that is constructed brick by brick, so is your personal and professional reputation. "Character is like a tree, and reputation like its shadow," said Charles Haddon Spurgeon. "The shadow is what we think of it; the tree is the real thing."

You are *not* your business. Although your company may bear your name, it is not you or who you are. Too many people are unable to separate themselves from their endeavor and mistakenly equate their businesses as an extension of themselves. Their emotions and their self-esteem rise and fall with the fortunes of their company. Consequently, they are unable to make clear-headed, unemotional decisions that are beneficial to its health.

Whether your company is doing well or not, the ability to set yourself apart from it enables you to always get the big picture. It is only when you can stand back and take a bird's eye view that you can observe the mountains and valleys ahead. As you go about your daily business activities, always look at the general scenery, keeping the horizon and your goals in sight ahead of you.

"It is better to be first in the mind than in the market," declare Ries and Trout in **The 22 Immutable Laws of Marketing**. The strategy is called positioning and it is what you want to achieve for your business or company. It means that you need to discover what your niche is in the marketplace and claim it as your own. Guard it fiercely and maintain it to the best of your abilities with both of your feet firmly planted on the ground.

The difference between public relations and advertising is simply dollars. Advertising is what you *pay* for to inform the world about you and your company on the air, television, or a Web site, in a magazine, newspaper, or other printed matter. Publicity is *free* or relatively inexpensive, created through news releases, granting interviews, television, writing articles, teaching courses and seminars, authoring books, speaking engagements and other promotional activities. You are the creator and keeper of the image that you want to project in the market or public's mind.

Maintaining good public relations brings recognition to you and your company, and requires diligence and follow through. Think of it as the marathon, not a short sprint. Stay in contact with the reporters and writers who interview you and keep them informed with regular media releases about your activities. Be sure to keep your alumni magazines (of each university you attended) and especially your local, community newspapers on the mailing list to receive such information. Don't overlook your chamber of commerce or your civic organization, which usually publishes a business journal, newsletter and bulletins.

Are you speaking at a conference or to an association? What have you published lately? Have you been featured on a television or radio program, or in newly-released books, journals or articles? Don't hide your accomplishments. Get the word out, regularly and consistently to all your business associates, customers, clients, friends, and relatives. Don't be shy about self-promotion as long as it is done in good taste and with professionalism.

Learn the power of a well-written media release and reap its benefits. Be helpful and courteous to members of the media and establish a good working relationship with them. If you don't know how to generate a strong press release yourself, you may find yourself paying up to $200 for someone else to write one for you. If you don't know how to get yourself on a radio or television show, you will find that it will cost from $100 to over $5,000 to pay a public relations firm or event management service to do so. Even then, there is no guarantee that you will be on the air. Any interview or taping could be eliminated by an editor for a variety of reasons.

Develop a marketing plan to go hand in hand with your business plan. This could be as simple as setting aside some time each day to call customers on the telephone, attend a trade show or convention, or distributing small giveaway items imprinted with your company's name. There are many forms of marketing, from no-cost word of mouth to direct mail to event sponsorship. Look into all of them to ascertain which fit your business and needs. My double-sided business card is always well-received because on the back are printed the dates of the next twelve Chinese New Years and their corresponding zodiac animals. I know that people will keep my card in their wallets for a *dozen* years because they need to refer to it. Consider what you could give away that people will keep around for a long time. Whatever the promotional item is, the longer people keep it, the longer your advertising is working for you and your company.

Establish a specific goal and budget for your marketing and advertising efforts, and comparison shop for an agency, artist, designer, or copywriter with whom you can work. Research carefully and choose wisely before spending any money on advertising. Those dollars can go quickly in large amounts.

Code all promotions and advertisements so that you can track and analyze their effectiveness. Use good common sense, and don't throw good money after the bad. If you are not getting results from your advertising or marketing dollars in a particular publication or medium, re-evaluate and spend your hard-earned dollars elsewhere that will bring payback or return.

I am invited to speak at many different conferences and conventions on a variety of subjects nationwide. Although some of them pay their speakers, many do not. It is believed that the exposure at the event should be adequate compensation for the speaker whose bio appears in the program and who can make valuable contacts. That means that I would have to pay my own expenses to deliver that speech or be on a panel.

Once I spent approximately $500 out-of-pocket for travel expenses and accommodations to present at the Urban Land Institute's spring meeting in Cleveland. Although there were over 2,000 attendees, fewer than forty attended the panel discussion focusing on multi-ethnic markets. However, my book **TARGET: The U.S. Asian Market** was displayed prominently in the conference bookstore in the foyer. It was seen and purchased by the president of a New York real estate company that owned a large, upscale shopping center in Long Island. Within two weeks, he had contacted me and contracted both my consulting and sales and marketing training services, resulting in one of my most interesting and profitable jobs.

Only you have the best idea and intuition about which jobs to accept and which to decline. Consider everything from the financial to the non-financial aspects of the work you take on. It may generate many sales, but you don't want to kill yourself in the process! It may be a huge contract or order, but the stress of dealing with an obnoxious, meddling client may cause your mental, psychological, and physical health to suffer. (See more about Clients from Hell in **Secret Number 12**.)

Coasting: Taking Care of Business

SECRET NUMBER 9

The Company You Keep

**You can't fly like an eagle
when you're surrounded by turkeys.**

-Anonymous

E ach year I travel all over the country delivering speeches and facilitating intercultural training seminars to a range of audiences in many different settings. I've been to a dozen states just in the last forty-eight months and relish the opportunity to hear other professional speakers at their craft. When asked to speak at conferences, I always take the time to mingle and converse with the attendees so that I can begin my remarks with a comment or two that relates to them.

On one occasion, a close friend and I had traveled separately to present at the same conference being held in Scottsdale, Arizona at the Camelback Inn. The luncheon speaker on the first day was a brash, fast-talking woman whose topic was "How to Get Along with Difficult People." While her style and most of her message was rather unsophisticated for the largely citified audience, she made one point that stuck in my mind.

"Surround yourself with happy people," she told us. The concept was and is a simple one, and yet, the more I thought about it, the more profound it was. Recently, another person brought up a similar point. "Angi," she told me, "you can always hire technical competence and brilliance, but a happy, enthusiastic employee is beyond price."

There is a lot of truth in her remark. The people you surround yourself with are your reference group. It is important to hire applicants who are happy and appreciate having a job. Just about anybody can be trained or empowered with specialized skills, but a positive attitude (or a sunny disposition) is priceless. If you ever come across any person who possesses it in abundance, hire her or him before someone else does!

The same holds true for the people with whom you associate other than those in your company. If you hang around successful businesspeople, their ways of thinking and operating will rub off on you. Read their publications, learn and practice their methods, and hear them speak. Be like a mirror and reflect their sunny light and prosperity.

On the other hand, if you are constantly in the company of negative and pessimistic folks, you too, will be affected. Make a conscious effort to avoid this kind of person as much as you can. Negativism is like an insidious poison that infects everyone. You get dragged down. It can devastate morale and wreak havoc on efficiency and productivity.

How do you determine which of many applicants will be good employees? Ask them a lot of questions and listen carefully to their responses. Does the person share your ideals, goals, and vision? Which is more important to you: experience, knowledge, or attitude? A survey of CEOs of major corporations indicated that attitude, and not technical knowledge, is considered the most significant attribute sought in an employee.

My friend Bill Chiang told me that he selects his employees on the basis of the Rae Thompson Test. Rae was the Alphagraphics print shop owner who sold him the business and who had a unique way of evaluating job applicants. When a job seeker arrived for his or her interview, Rae would make a point of meeting that person near the front entrance of the store.

After introductions were made, Rae would turn around and briskly walk straight back to her small office at the rear of the store. At the same time, she would observe *how* the applicant followed her. She discovered that generally one of two things would happen. A few of the applicants kept the pace she set and would be right behind her all the way, but for the most part, the others would lag behind, creating a large gap between them.

Rae hired the few who followed her lead and her speed. She figured that those applicants communicated their sharpness and readiness by their willingness to keep the pace she set. Conversely, those who did not, indicated by their manner that they were either unwilling or unable to follow a leader.

It was an interesting and unscientific method of assessment, but Rae claims that it was a very accurate one. The people she put to the test and hired turned out to be very good, dependable, and loyal employees who worked at her store for years.

While you cannot pay someone to have a good attitude, you can certainly hire someone who has one. Surround yourself with joyful people who appreciate want to work and who love their jobs. This one trait may prove to be more valuable to your company than superior technical skills. You can always train a new employee, but a cheerful outlook on life, flexibility, enthusiasm, optimism, love of learning and doing new things are priceless assets in my book. When you come across one of these uplifting people, try to find a place in your organization for them.

Martin Seligman of Metlife conducted a study in which he hired applicants who had failed the aptitude test but had high levels of optimism. After the first year, this group of people had made 21 percent more in sales and by the second year, produced 57 percent more.

A man is judged by the company he keeps. With whom do you associate outside your work environment? Who are your friends and business associates? Are they positive and successful role models, happily working? Do they hold highly responsible positions in their companies? Or they perhaps are just good, solid citizens with great dignity and character whom you admire and respect deeply? Have you surrounded yourself with people of different ethnicities, age groups, religious and spiritual beliefs to strengthen and expand the diversity in your own thinking? Are there folks around you on whom you can count on for friendship, fellowship, emotional and moral support?

Having an enduring and supportive circle of friends and family around you protects you from life's trials and is a major factor in keeping you healthy. For example, studies conducted with bone marrow transplant patients, men under emotional stress, and women who had advanced breast cancer, all showed a dramatic link between the healing power of emotional support.

Essentially, people, who have emotional support, live healthier and longer lives than those who are isolated, hostile, or angry. Living alone is not detrimental, for example, as long as you feel that you have the support you want when you need it. It is those who feel the gloom and darkness of hopelessness, futility, and despair who will suffer the most.

Protect yourself from suffering the negative effects of stress by learning to switch off your production of adrenaline when you don't need it. It's important for you to avoid cardiovascular disease and other illnesses by managing your anger, frustration, irritation, excitement and challenge. Give yourself time to recover by balancing the highs with the lows. Even mountain climbers get altitude sickness when they've been up in the higher elevations for long periods of time!

Would you believe that the empowerment of entrepreneurship is beneficial to your good health and contributes to your longevity? A recent study reported on KNX radio reported on a research project which followed the lives of 5,700 men for a period of twenty-one years. Those who did not have much control of their lives at work died at an earlier age than those who had control over decisions at their jobs.

Learn to bring balance into all aspects of your life and the healthier mind and body that result will have a positive effect on all of your endeavors.

SECRET NUMBER 10

Your People

**In the end, all business operations can be
reduced to three words: People, product,
profits. People come first.**

-Lee Ioccoca

I have seen this sign hanging on the walls of some businesses I patronize: If we don't take care of our customers, someone else will. The Chinese perceive the marketplace to be a battlefield on which wars are won or lost and are therefore taught military strategies that could be applied to the economic battlefield, too. Every business grows, one client at a time. When you are just starting out and during the first few years of your company, you will remember many of those initial clients and the service you provided or the product that you sold to them.

In every business, people should come first. There are only two kinds to concern yourself with. The first is your employees; the second are your customers.

I learned a lot from my dad when I was growing up in Washington, D.C. He got his orders to return to Taiwan just about the time I was finishing high school, and resigned so that he and Mom could remain in the United States while I continued my university education.

At first Dad worked in a Chinese restaurant in D.C.'s one-block Chinatown, but later he and several of his old pals from China partnered together to found several Chinese restaurants. There were eventually three of them: a Good Earth in nearby

Virginia, one in New Carrollton, Maryland, and Grand China in Rockville, Maryland.

Himself an old-timer, or *wha kiew* (overseas Chinese), Dad did things the old-fashioned way. Before he became a diplomat, he had studied at Wharton School of Business at the University of Pennsylvania, and returned to China to establish a freight company. Later as a restaurateur, manager and partner, he did everything, from picking up lint off the carpet, meeting and greeting customers, staffing the tiny bar and mixing drinks, and making deposits in the bank's night drop after hours.

One thing that he did that impressed me the most was that every day he would drive from our home in Northwest D.C. all the way to downtown to pick up the cook and several waiters and drive them out to Maryland.   At night, he did the reverse, taking them all home so that he himself would arrive home close to midnight.

He was a father to every one who worked with and for him: kind, compassionate, fair, and caring. He took care of his employees and they paid him back with loyalty a thousandfold. Fifteen years later, when he finally sold the Good Earth and retired, several of the original waiters and waitresses were still there. Dad had seen them through many of the milestones of their lives

Your customers are what create your business. Meeting their needs is what you need to learn to do best. In my book **TARGET: The U.S. Asian Market,** *A Practical Guide to Doing Business*, I quote the following research statistics:

- 96% of unhappy customers never complain
- 91% of dissatisfied customers take their business elsewhere
- 82% of customers are lost to poor performance or bad attitude

Think about yourself as a customer. Shouldn't you expect courtesy, respect, dignity, and professionalism at any place you patronize or with whom you do business? Do you reward the people and places you like by continuing to give them your business? Do you return to a restaurant or store or service at which you have had a bad experience? Surely you are not a glutton for punishment! I daresay that most of us never go back to a business at which we have been treated shabbily or spoken to rudely.

There are millions of businesses out there, folks. Your customers have chosen you from among all of them. Do what you can and have to , to exceed their expectations and retain them. After all, it's a real horse race, but there's an important lesson to be learned at the race track. The horse that wins very often does so by only a nose. And remember the difference between the first place purse and the second-place purse can be hundreds of thousands, perhaps even millions of dollars. It's the same lesson at a golf tournament or at the Olympics: the champion wins by just fractions of inches or seconds. You can be on the cutting edge of your business by just being that much better than your competition, by making the 125 percent effort instead of just getting the job done.

Many people settle for being mediocre and getting by with a minimum amount of effort. Those who are successful as entrepreneurs are more likely than not, willing to go the extra distance for their customers and clients. They are like those winning horses, and yet the difference is great between the champion horse and the second-place winner.

Capitalize on what you do well and exceed your customer's expectations. Under-promise and over-deliver. Overestimate and come in under budget. Why can't every businessperson return phone calls within 48 hours or less? Why should it take two to four weeks for merchandise to reach you when you order something by mail? Why can't you handle your customer complaints expediently? Entrepreneurs excel in eliminating "can't" from their vocabularies and ask "Why not?"

The entrepreneur who gives his or her very best effort to providing the most outstanding service, quality, and value will stand out from the crowd. It's not difficult to do at all. People today have lowered their standards and expectations and have settled for much less than they deserve. It makes me feel great when I hear, "Thank you so much for getting back to me so quickly." And it never fails to puzzle me because the person sounds so surprised. It's pretty curious that the current spate of new books in the business section of bookstores deal with the subject of customer service. It indicates that either we have lost the knack of taking care of our customers and have to learn or re-learn how to do it. Perhaps many businesspeople don't know how to provide that exceptional service because they themselves have rarely experienced it. Whatever the reasons, if you provide better service and quality than the next guy, you can't go wrong. The word will get around soon enough.

Keep in touch with your customers. There are many ways to do this—courtesy phone calls, holiday greeting cards (Thanksgiving is a great time), small gifts, lunches, discounts, etc. One of the things that I have done is to keep my eyes and ears open for publications and articles that I think would be of interest to my clients. One of them, for example, is a major homebuilder with a development right in my own community although his offices are over fifty miles away. Every time I see a feature or news item in the local rag that pertains to education or the quality of life, I clip and send it to him with a short note. It costs me only a few minutes to keep in touch with him this way, but he appreciates having the most current information with which to market his new homes.

Take good care of your customers and they will take care of you. The old 80/20 rule is one example. It states that 80 percent of your business will be generated by only 20 percent of your customers. Speaking of 20, it takes twenty times more effort to get a new customer than to get a referral from a past customer. Last but not least, it costs ten times more money to get a new customer than to service an existing customer.

Again, there is a lesson here. It helps you decide to take care of the important things first, to prioritize your activities and to decide whose telephone calls you should return before all others. It makes things simple. When you collect all your messages from your voice mail or secretary, scan them first and prioritize them right then and there. Give precedence to your existing customers. Then call the prospective clients and customers. At the bottom of the totem pole should be those that are neither important nor urgent.

There are many ways to keep track of your messages without losing them. You may have an electronic personal secretary that connects with your personal computer which then downloads all your messages and prints everything out. There are a wide variety of different personal organizers, appointment books and telephone message systems to choose from.

The method I use is definitely low-tech, but works for me because I deplore spending hours in front of my computer. All of my telephone messages are jotted down as I retrieve them, on plain white 8-1/2" x 11" copy paper. The date written and circled in the top right corner. Then I listen to and record each message in pencil and draw a line across the page at the end of that entry. The unlined paper allows me to use as much or little space as needed for each person's remarks, which could be long or short.

When I return the message, I add notes *in ink* during the conversation   to fill in the details and other pertinent and important information. If I left a message for that person, sent a fax, or mailed printed material, I make notations such as "LM" or "fax" and the date to the left of his or her name. Completed calls are marked with a large check using a highlighter near the left edge. At a glance, I can immediately tell to whom I have answered calls and what action was taken.

Of course, there will be times when I have called all but one or two names from the page. These I mark with the same colored marker with a long dash on the left side as a reminder that I cannot retire this message page until it's taken care of. When the all persons listed on the page have been checked off, the paper is then filed chronologically in a three-hole punch loose-leaf binder. The more important names and numbers are then added to my database for the future.

As I recognize myself as a visual learner, this method works extremely well for me. All of my ongoing projects are stored in 3" loose-leaf binders with labels on their spines: Projects in progress, prospects, telephone messages, speech notes, research notes, completed projects January through June, finished projects from July through December just about everything. The index tabs for current projects serve well as the file dividers in the notebooks at the end of each year when I empty them all out and turn all files, contracts, and related correspondence sideways, retiring them to storage boxes. The box for the most recent past year is kept nearby for handy reference; older files are put into less accessible storage.

Avoid telephone tag. There is nothing more useless, frustrating and non-productive than hearing or leaving a message that says So and So called. Whether you leave a message with an electronic or live message-taker, make every one count by being *productive*. Tell the person your reason for calling, the best times to reach you during the next two days, and then make a point to be available when the call comes through. When the two of you are trying to set up an appointment, but you're both very busy, leave some actual dates and times that you're available. This will give enough information for your contact to check his/her calendar and get back to you to confirm your meeting. In other words, move things along by leaving constructive, informative messages that facilitate action and progress.

Follow through. If you meet someone and say that you will send or fax something or do something, be certain that you do so right away. Take care of the details so that they don't trip you up down the line. Don't leave any loose ends, especially if you have to leave town. Always call in for your messages daily while you're away as well as return them. People will be impressed when you tell them that you're returning their call from a distant city. It shows that you care about them, are responsive, and in charge.

One last word about people. Because you are a person of honesty, integrity and character, you may believe the same of others. Unfortunately, this is not so. I was rudely reminded of this recently when I discovered that someone had withdrawn a large amount of money from my checking account. It was taken by forgery on "paper transactions" from various branch locations. I was advised to call up the Social Security Administration, all the department stores, gasoline and credit card companies for which I had cards and to inquire if anyone had requested extra. A police report had to be filed.

Once someone has your checking account and social security numbers, he can access a great deal of personal information about you. Destroy all unused checkbooks, deposit slips, old financial records, even unsolicited credit card offers in your name which arrive in the mail. Lock up all your personal bank records, new and cancelled checks, and credit card purchase slips of your customers so that no one can get information from them. Guard all information about yourself and your customers and be cautious as to how and where you dispose of your trash.

Better to be safe than sorry.

SECRET NUMBER 11

Word of Mouth

The Rule of 99:
One satisfied (or unhappy) customer will
relate his experience to others who will
repeat it until eventually 99 people will
have heard about the incident.
-Anonymous

There is a party game called Gossip in which the participants sit in a circle or make a line. The first person makes a statement to the next who in turn whispers the information to the third, and so on, until the last person declares what has been passed on to him. In every case, the final announcement does not resemble the first in any way. The game is meant to illustrate how a simple remark can be totally misconstrued or distorted in its retelling until it is unrecognizable.

In business, word of mouth is very much like the game Gossip. A customer experiences either a good or bad experience when doing business with you and your company, and relates it to others. Research has shown that the story will be repeated over and over until ultimately, 99 people have heard it, thus the name "The Rule of 99."

A White House Office of Consumer Affairs study found that an unhappy customer will most likely share his unhappiness with at least nine others. 13 percent of these folks will tell their grievances to *more than 20* other people. This form of communication, then, is most likely to be negative, but it is as Chip Walker in *American Demographics* calls it, "a voluntary exchange of referrals, techniques, tips, war stories, and anecdotes."

Some time ago, I had planned a full-day workshop on targeting and reaching the Asian market at the Four Seasons Hotel in Newport Beach, California. Months ahead of time, I had called and mailed my deposit to secure a conference room. On the day of the workshop, I arrived at the hotel over an hour early, as is my habit, to prepare the room for the attendees. With a bellhop in tow pulling along my visual aids and handouts on a luggage carrier, I made my way toward the assigned room.

As we neared the room, we could hear voices coming from within, and a peek through the crack between the double doors confirmed my worst suspicions. The room had been assigned to and was occupied by the representatives of a local bank. A call to the banquet manager resulted in a reassignment of my room to another on a high floor with panoramic views. At the conclusion of the workshop, I returned to my office to write a letter immediately to the banquet manager of the hotel.

Relating the scenario and the aggravation and anxiety that it caused me, I told her how unhappy I was with my experience at that world-class, four-star hotel. Not too long afterwards, I received a letter of apology and an offer to conduct my next workshop there free of charge.

Since that experience, I have told this story to many people, maybe the statistical nine, or even twenty. The story always ends on a positive note about the manager's offer. A savvy businesswoman, she did not jeopardize the sterling reputation of the hotel for the mere several hundred dollars charge for using a conference room. It's quite possible that you have had a similar negative occurrence in your life and have told your friends and associates about it. This is exactly how the principle of word of mouth works.

Remember that every business starts out with just one customer or a client, large or small, and grows little by little, or by leaps and bounds. Most business start-ups do not have the budget to spend on advertising, so word of mouth is the most cost-effective method way of establishing your reputation. Whatever you do, whether it be manufacturing a product or providing a service, do it right and the best you can *the first time*. It's easy to tell when you have a satisfied customer; it's the one who thanks you!

Don't let a marketing opportunity escape, when you hear those magic words "Thank you." It is the most opportune moment for you to respond by saying, "I appreciate your business/patronage. As you are happy with the work that we've done for you (or the service/product we've provided), may I give you my business card so you can refer/mention us to your friends, family and associates?" Give your pleased customer *several* of your cards to distribute to his or her circle.

During the first five years of my consulting and training business, I tracked how each new client found me. I charted every new client or prospect to discover who was passing along my name to other companies. Even today, when someone calls me for the first time, I religiously ask, "From whom did you get my name?" Making a note of the reply, I made it standard practice to write a letter of thanks to that person for the referral, sometimes even obtaining the names and addresses from my new contact.

Tracking the responses is an important method for finding out the effectiveness of your marketing effort. Whatever is working well, whether it be by word of mouth, advertising, public relations direct mail, cold calling, or referrals, you need to know how to improve and expand on it. Discard those that haven't produced results by constantly evaluating and analyzing. You can't afford to do otherwise.

Common sense tells you that if your advertising dollars are not producing, you shouldn't throw good money after the bad and renew an ad. If a promotion was successful, not only in attracting a lot of traffic to your business, but created sales, you should repeat or develop it. If speaking at a meeting, convention or conference generated prospects and clients, you might consider doing more of the same.

Sometimes you have to weigh the advantages and disadvantages of each method. Do you have the time or expertise, for example, to regularly generate media releases to keep your name in the local print and electronic media, or will you have to pay someone to do it for you? You may consider whether or not you want to spend the money for listing your name and business in the many trade or media directories that are published annually.

In my business of intercultural consulting and training and publishing, it is money well spent to be listed in several of these because inclusion keeps my name and business visible or "out there." I am the only name listed, for example, in some of them under *feng shui*, the Chinese environmental art of placement. As this is a topic that is beginning to gain national attention, my half-page ad will be quietly working for me, day in and day out, even during the times I am not actively marketing. The ad positions me as a resource person who is available for interviews on the subject.

I found that referrals have come from current and former clients, workshop participants, secretaries, friends, associates, and members of my many audiences have given my name and number out to others. Some calls have come from people who kept my business card for several years before contacting me for advice or to do work for them.

Word of mouth is the cheapest form of marketing you can use for your service or product, compared to advertising in print or electronic media which can cost a bundle of bucks. Your reputation as a businessperson and the impact of what people say about you and your business can literally, make or break you. When people hear positive things about you, your position and standing are reinforced.

How smoothly, responsibly, effectively, responsively, and profitably you organize yourself and your business creates your image and establishes your reputation. You should never compromise your integrity, reputation or character. As Thomas Jefferson said, "In matters of principle, stand like a rock; in matters of taste, swim with the current." What goes around, comes around. Reap what you sow. If you do an outstanding job in the service that you provide or the product you create, your business will grow and prosper.

If you are greedy or less than ethical, it will eventually come back to haunt you in one form or another. "Man's many desires are like the small metal coins he carries about in his pocket," said Satya Sai Baba, "the more he has the more they weigh him down." Remember that the bitterness of poor quality remains long after the sweetness of low price is forgotten.

Your work is your signature. The Chinese have a saying: Of a dead leopard we keep the skin...of man his reputation. What have you heard said about other people or yourself? Once a friend asked me for the name of a public relations person that she could use on a project. The name I gave her drew this response, "Oh no, that person's fees are too high because I understand she pads them." Another time, I mentioned the name of an architect to my uncle, asking if he knew him. "Yes, I do, but he writes his contracts for one amount and by the time the job is done, the costs have gone up considerably because he adds a lot of unexpected expenses," In other words, the architect did not come in under his clients' budgets and it was well known.

What will your reputation be? It is what you make it, constructing it brick by brick, client by client. To build it will take a hundred years; to destroy it only a day. If you are at fault, admit it. Few will remember the wrong; most will remember your courage.

"To thine own self be true," Shakespeare told us. Building on your abilities, strengths, and what you do best allows you to do them well and with vigor and enthusiasm, simply because success breeds success. No doubt you will discover that some activities or products that you take on are beyond your scope, but you may still do them for the money or the experience. In the past, I have facilitated focus groups and statistical market research, finding them to be very labor-intensive and unsatisfying. I know that I do not have the training to conduct diversity training and therefore refer requests for that type of project to those with the proper professional expertise.

Recently, a prospect met with me to discuss engaging my services to assist him in negotiating with his Japanese clients. It would have been a plum of a job, but I knew in my heart that guiding him through complex negotiations was beyond both my scope and expertise. To accept the job, as eager as he was to hire me to help him, I felt, would have been fraudulent, and I told him so. After declining his offer graciously, I told him that I would be happy to forward to him the names of my associates who were experts in the field.

"I appreciate your honesty," he said, "it is so refreshing." That one statement validated my feeling that I had done the right thing.

SECRET NUMBER 12

Clients from Hell

Some money is not worth making.
-Sammy Loh

S ooner or later, the inevitable will happen. It may occur in your fifth day of business, fifth year, or the fifteenth year. Almost every entrepreneur I've met has had the experience,   one that everybody shudders with the retelling, and nobody wishes to repeat. The names and the places may differ, but the stories are mythical in their similarities. You will finally meet your first Client from Hell.

Luckily, in the hundreds of business transactions and activities with which I've been involved through the years as an entrepreneur, I have only had two of these. The first was a builder in a small town in Northern California for whom I had made the air trip to assess his development. I was to make suggestions as well as write a report on how to improve its appeal to the Asian homebuyer.

After spending an entire day performing the scope of work as outlined in the signed consulting contract, I sent him the detailed report followed by the invoice for my services and expenses. When the payment arrived, he had shortchanged me by four hundred dollars. Enclosed was a note saying that the quality of my work did not deem the full payment.

I evaluated the report and came to the conclusion that it was a quality piece and that the client was really trying to cheat me. (As you may find out, some will; others are just damn cheap or downright unethical.) My heart and gut told me that I should go after this guy to recover my due just as a matter of principle. The main question was whether it was worth it to do so.

Was my client a major player in the building industry and would it be worth it to provoke or agitate him? Would my reputation be at stake if I did? Would my subsequent actions kill my chances of ever doing business in the region again?

Consulting with several of my developer friends in Southern California about the situation helped me to decide what to do next. One of my pals had a cousin who was also a builder in the town where my client was located and he offered to find out information for me.

Within two days, I received a call from my friend.

"My cousin says that the guy is a small-time builder who only builds a few homes a year," came the word. I thanked him and decided then and there to let it go. I felt strongly that it wasn't worth either my time or money to pursue the issue. Some of you may say, "But you lost several hundred dollars!" Yes, that may be so, but as a believer in losing the battle to win the war, I chose to cut my losses and focus my attention on more important clients and projects.

That little experience was small potatoes compared to the only *real* Client from Hell I met in 1995. This one was a major advertising company owned by off-shore interests, in fact, one of the largest in the world. The rep called me up and told me that someone had referred me to his company to do some work for them. I was honored and flattered because it was one of the biggest jobs I had ever been offered. I was contracted to conduct eight focus groups to determine the feasibility and profitability of a new product, specifically, organic tofu. (Okay, you non-Californians can stop laughing now. I know, I know, the whole concept is *so* California.) I felt confident that I could plan and implement the project and proceeded.

To make a long story short, it was simply the worst experience in all my years as a businesswoman. Although the first half of the project went without a hitch, the remainder was the stuff of my worst nightmares. The three-month project, which began in October, dragged on for eight months, bringing me down with it. The client began making changes in the scope of work and their expectations were constantly changing. The company began demanding all sorts of things such as a written report when verbally they had told me that none was required. The phone calls to my office were coming at the rate of several of day, asking for this and that. *Nothing* I did could please them. It was like trying to shoot a moving target from a train!

Providing outstanding customer service has always been one of my top priorities, so I persevered, making every effort to accommodate the client, even though I knew I was stretching the limits of the provisions of my contract. This one job was becoming so time, labor, and attention-intensive, that it dominated my life. Fortunately, I still had the stamina to service my other clients at the same time, but the effort was beginning to take its toll. The situation caused me so much stress that I couldn't eat or sleep. A racing heart and high anxiety were my constant companions.

In the midst of the maelstrom, someone said to me, "That's the biggest client you've ever had; won't you do anything for them?"

Normally, I would have said yes, but by this time it was April. In less than a heartbeat, I had my answer.

"No," I replied, "that's called prostitution." At that very moment, I realized that I had to extricate myself or ruin my health and possibly my business. I could no longer permit this client to run me to the ground. The last straw came when I received the final payment for the work I had done for them. The Client from Hell had shortchanged me four thousand dollars.

In a civil, concise letter, I informed them that I would take them to court for the amount they owed me. After we exchanged several phone calls, they sent me half of it. As in the first scenario, I let the remainder go. Sure, it was two thousand dollars, but once again, I decided that my time, health, and energy were valuable and not to be wasted further on this particular client. It was time to cut loose, get on with my life, and I did.

You, too, will meet your nemesis someday, the client about whom you will tell horror stories for years to come. The one who thinks he or she owns you, body and soul, just because you provide a business service. That person is usually a control freak, intimidating and mean-spirited, wanting to demonstrate his or her power over you, time and time again. Very often, the person may be obscenely wealthy, although rudeness, crudeness, and pettiness is not the exclusive domain of the affluent. Clients from Hell come in all shapes and sizes, all ages and ethnicities, and in all businesses.

A friend of mine who manages a business that custom-designs and constructs very expensive, imported European kitchens told me the story about one of these people. At a job site, he witnessed a woman who confronted her housekeeper. Ordering the young woman to follow her, the client made her way to a cavernous, walk-in wardrobe, demanding to know what was wrong with the clothes.

Everything appeared to be in order: skirts, blouses, dresses, jackets, coats, and other items were organized, grouped and neatly arranged according to color and season. The woman kept repeating the question, her voice becoming louder and shriller.

"Tell me what's wrong with the clothes!" she screamed.

The hapless maid looked around carefully, clearly puzzled and in a dilemma, as she couldn't see anything out of place or order.

The woman, in her rage, then reached up and pulled every single thing off every shelf and rack, creating a jumbled mess on the floor. Then she commanded that the girl put everything back. Neither my friend nor the maid ever discovered what was wrong with the clothes.

Nothing you do or say will be good enough for your Client from Hell. Your work, designs, ideas—whatever you are doing for this monster—will never satisfy him or her. The client delights in having you at his or her beck and call all the time, calling and faxing instructions to you during the days, evenings, and even on weekends. You will lose control of your life because this person will micromanage every minute of it. You will experience heart palpitations and even anxiety attacks. You will be living a nightmare during your waking hours.

How much will you be able to take? Is your self-esteem and confidence strong enough to take such shabby treatment from another human being? Will you be able to maintain your dignity and tell the client to stuff it and just take your losses? Imagine what you would do if one of your employees is on the receiving end of such behavior.

Imagine this scenario. At some point, you will have to take a stand up to this person. What will be the straw that will break your back? Is what the client paying you worth all the abuse you are subjected to? Is your health, mental and physical, up to the havoc the Client from Hell will wreak?

Be forewarned and prepared.

To be a businessperson, you must develop a thick skin. You cannot take everything personally or be too sensitive about every little comment or pettiness that you experience. Don't take criticism to heart. You can be sure that there are going to be days when everything goes well between you and your clients, and other days during which everybody and everything may rub you the wrong way. Learn to keep your composure and cultivate skills that enable you to deal effectively with obnoxious, offensive or irritating customers and clients.

Two friends of mine own a printing service and the husband is constantly amazed at how well his wife handles demanding, rude customers. His wife told him that it wasn't hard for her to smile and stay pleasant. After all, she says, those e pay their bills and their two daughters' tuition at rivate school.

It also takes wisdom on your part to know which of your employees would be best at handling the public. Of course, all those in your employ share your vision and goals, but certain personalities handle complaints and the public better than others. Look for those cool, controlled, strong types who can remain unruffled in the worst of circumstances, rather than an emotional being who would just add fuel to the fire. Remember that when one is fire (or all fired up), the other must be water. Hopefully, the water person will be your employee who can soothe the raging beasts.

Other Clients from Hell are those who don't or won't pay you. It's a fine line for all of us entrepreneurs to walk when, on one hand, we need to collect from our customers, while on the other hand, we don't want to chase them away. One $2 million business found that 45 percent of its payments averaged over 30 days late.

As a small business, how can you get a handle on collections before it becomes overwhelming? Take the offensive and be proactive. Don't wait until 60 or 90 days after the invoice was first issued before taking action. First of all, you should know who your customers are. If a new customer comes to you by referral, it would be a good bet. You may call up the referring party and investigate the prospect before you take on the job. Build in a 1 per cent late charge for each month the bill remains unpaid.

Don't wait a month to bill your customers. Send invoices every two or three weeks. For those of you who provide business services, construct your contract so that you get paid a percentage to begin the scope of work, another as it is in progress, and the balance at its conclusion.   If your business is a product, get at least a partial payment up front, which will ensure that you aren't left with a bundle of out-of-pocket expenses.   Motivate your sales and collections staffs with commissions and incentives.

If a month has passed with no payment in sight, it's time to launch your telephone campaign.   Start with a friendly call and say something like, "I know that you're busy, and it's probably an oversight, but your invoice of ___(date)__ has not been paid yet.   When can we expect to receive it?" You'll probably get any of a number of excuses so be sure to fax a copy of the bill right then and there. Right after the call, put that same bill stamped with PAST DUE and a short note mentioning your conversation in the mail.

Now it's a couple of weeks later and you still haven't received anything.   Make a second call to find out what has caused the delay and ask how "we" can help to resolve the matter, perhaps even suggesting alternative ways of payment, such as in increments or by accepting in-kind services.

While you are waiting for a response, consider your next moves: a lawyer's letter on letterhead stationery demanding the money or engaging the services of a collection agency, both of which will start costing you money. A collection agency typically will charge a 30 percent commission and collect less than twenty-five cents on the dollar.   Lawsuits are expensive and time-consuming, so think long and hard and don't be too eager to sue. There's no rule of thumb about how much you can afford to lose as litigation itself is costly. Ask yourself if it is worth your time, money, and energy to pursue this last resort. If, after four months you still have not collected, cut your losses and move on.

What are some basic strategies for preventing complaints? The first is good listening skills. Asking questions that require thoughtful responses will enable you to get honest feedback from your clients and customers. By meeting their needs, you can eliminate complaints in the first place. But if somebody is finding fault with your service or product, listen carefully and actively in order to discover how you can best resolve the situation. Make a point to listen more than you speak when dealing with an irate customer. Ask frequent, clarifying questions and avoid jumping to conclusions or forming your response until the person has finished speaking.

When confronted with an emotional person, acknowledge the emotion with statements such as, "I understand how you are feeling angry/frustrated/annoyed/etc. and I want to help you," and "What would you do in my position that you feel would be fair to everyone concerned?"

Don't get dragged down into argumental quicksand. Your responsibility is to solve the problem, not add to it. Do your very best to keep your composure and do not take the complaint personally. Attack the problem vigorously, but not the people responsible.

Many customers only need someone to listen to them attentively and sympathetically, and do not demand anything. Then there will also be others who will complain, whine, are aggressive or hostile, or who know it all. This latter group will not be placated, no matter how much time you spend with them or how long you listen. By narrowing your questioning, you can bring the exchange into your control.

On the other hand, there will be times when the proverbial shoe will be on the other foot and fairness and principle will be tested. It may have nothing to do with people. You will encounter situations that challenge your integrity and sense of justice and those will be the moments when you should be firm and take a stand for what you believe is good, truthful, and right.

Remember that as a businessperson, you too, are someone else's customer and that you deserve quality, value, and courtesy. If you feel that you have been treated poorly or have a legitimate complaint, you need to let the management know about it. Do not suffer in silence or the problem will never have the chance to be corrected. Take the few extra moments to complete and submit comment cards supplied by various businesses that you patronize, or sit down and write a letter.

The several times when I pointed out substandard service or quality to those responsible or in charge, they were always appreciative of hearing about it and for the opportunity to make things right. All were taken care of promptly and professionally, leaving me with a positive impression. After all, they were practicing the Rule of 99.

The first time happened shortly after I had purchased a new laser printer made by a major manufacturer of business machines. For over a month I contended with all sorts of glitches that I tried to adjust by reading the manual. Finally, in exasperation, I called the toll-free number to get assistance. Either I could not get through because the line was busy or was put on hold for a long period each time I tried to reach technical assistance.

After several frustrating efforts, I got on my computer to compose and send a short but pointed letter addressed to the president of the company whose address was listed in the printer's collateral materials.

First, I gave concise details regarding my purchase from an electronics franchise, then described the difficulties that I was experiencing. Next I told the executive about the inconvenience and how as a publisher, I prided myself in a 24-hour turnaround time to fill orders for our titles. This was followed by an account of how the equipment manufactured by his company was making me look unresponsive and unprofessional. Finally, taking a line from the announcements made by in-flight airline personnel at landings, I wrote, "I had a large selection of laser printers to choose from when I made my purchase and decided on yours because of its reputation. I am so unhappy with my decision that I am prepared to return it for a full refund and exchange it for printer made by another company."

A few days after I sent the letter, I received a call from the secretary from the regional president of the company. Within minutes of my answering the telephone, I was transferred to one of their technicians who instructed me on how to eliminate all the problems that I had been experiencing. I kept the printer and followed up with a thank you letter to the same person.

The second occurrence took place very recently. A reservation had been made for me at a hotel in Atlanta and I arrived to check in around three o'clock in the afternoon. I was given a pleasant room next to the elevator in which I left my luggage before leaving for the day's appointments.

When I arrived back around ten o'clock, I found much to my dismay, that I could hear the hydraulics and mechanism of the elevator every time it was used. In a fifteen-minute period alone, I counted over twenty ascents and descents. I called the front desk, describing the situation, explaining that the elevator was making so much noise that I would not be able to get a good night's sleep during my stay.

"I am conducting a day-long seminar tomorrow," I told the night desk clerk, "and it is imperative that I am properly rested."

"I'll check into it," the young man at the end of the line assured me, "and I'll get back to you."

I waited and waited for his response, even delaying my shower so as not to miss his call. It never came. Forty-five minutes later, I called him back and inquired on his progress.

"Any luck on my being moved to a quieter room?" I inquired.

"No, the hotel is full and nothing else is available."

Sure enough, my sleep was interrupted by the movement of the elevator all night. The next morning, I went downstairs to the front desk and asked for the manager.

When the man arrived, I asked if I could speak to him *privately* and if there was a quiet spot at which we could chat. We found a suitable location off the lobby and I told him about the room and the elevator.

"I checked in early enough and when there were other rooms available," I explained quietly and firmly. "There was no reason that I was given the room next to the elevator. When I called down to the front desk, I was told by the night desk clerk that I would be contacted. I waited and finally had to follow-up myself and still got stuck in that substandard room."

The manager responded that that particular room was usually assigned when the hotel was fully booked and only as a last resort. He then offered not to charge me for the room and I thanked him, feeling both vindicated and that the whole situation had been resolved fairly and satisfactorily.

My experience has been that an appropriate, unemotional but clear letter (or face-to-face meeting) addressed to the management will get positive results. It is important to do the following:

1) Direct your communication/concern to the top management, using the person's name and title if possible

2) Mention something positive first—about your trip, the city, the people—*anything* (Remember what Mary Poppins said about the spoonful of sugar and the medicine. Criticism will only be constructive if heard.)

3) Provide a clear, chronological description of the occurrence or situation. Keep your tone businesslike and professional. Begin with: *I am writing to inform you about my recent experience at your hotel/facility with your company's equipment/etc.* Or when seeking resolution in person: *May I speak to your manager...* (when (s)he shows up*)...I would like to speak with you privately please.* Use a calm, steady, soft voice.

4) State how the situation caused you to *feel* or *look* (to your clients). Use words like *unprofessional, dismay,*

mistaken, misinterpreted, anxiety, disappointed, distress ,etc.

5) Say: *As a fellow businessperson, you can appreciate....and I know that you would like to correct this situation.*

6) Suggest ways of "reasonable and fair" resolution that you would accept: return, exchange for a new one, not being charged for the room/car or whatever, a full refund, credit for future use.

7) Thank the person and say that you are pleased with the outcome and appreciate his/her help in settling the problem.

These guidelines have worked for me in many, diverse situations, and they are effective in facilitating positive solutions to a variety of complaints. Above all, keep in mind that your goal is to achieve a win-win situation for all concerned so that all parties involved can benefit.

Are We There Yet?

SECRET NUMBER 13

It's all in Your Head

**If you do not succeed, you have
been unsuccessful.
You are *not* a failure.**
-Overheard at a Venice Beach restaurant

It was the spring of 1996 when I met Suzanne Wickham-Beaird, the West Coast publicity director for Random House, for lunch to celebrate the publication of **Feng Shui: Arranging Your Home to Change Your Life**, for which I had authored the foreword. We were at a trendy restaurant on Market Street, half a block away from the famed Venice Beach, enjoying our meal when another group of diners was seated at a table right behind us.

Their conversation was loud and lively, and being a well-brought up diplomat's daughter, I tuned it out. The group could have been talking about business or sports or psychology, it really didn't matter as I was oblivious to its content. Suddenly out of the general hum, a man's voice rose clearly.

"If you try something, and you do not succeed," he declared to his companions, "it means that you were unsuccessful, not that you are a failure." This chance remark struck me in its simplicity and truth, and I have shared it with many people since.

As human beings first, and entrepreneurs second, all of us will experience triumphs and disappointments, achievements and setbacks, completion and frustration. Our character, self-motivation, zeal, persistence, passion, and a plethora of other attributes will drive us. When we stumble or topple, we will pick ourselves up, dust ourselves off, and keep moving to achieve our dreams and goals.

It will be difficult for you to be an entrepreneur and a pessimist. I think that we belong to the group of folks who have faith and are naturally confident. After all, would you have gone into business for yourself if you already believed it wouldn't succeed? If you are an optimist, you will chalk the fall to the situation, learn from it, and proceed. Promise yourself that you will not falter again, even as you pay more attention to your footing. Pessimists, on the other hand, are adept at blaming everything that happens on themselves, and worse yet, internalizing the feeling, thus reinforcing the negative so that it creates a vicious cycle.

When something you planned or did is unsuccessful, acknowledge that it was through no fault of yours. Do not take this setback personally by condemning yourself. There might have been many reasons that your project did not succeed: the market may not have been conducive; the timing may not have been right; public opinion may not have been on your side; society was just not ready for your brilliance.

Remember what I said earlier: you are *not* your business. If there are days or projects that do not meet your goals, if your company does not meet your expectations or is unsuccessful, resist the urge to feel or believe that it is a blow to *the person who you are*. In other words, do not permit feelings of inadequacy, frustration, loss, incompetency, uncertainty, and other destructive emotions to overwhelm you. (Alright, alright, you may feel sorry for yourself for up to a day and no more.)

The word responsibility is the *ability to respond*. We are the master of our emotions and have control over what we feel and subsequently do about them. If you have any doubt about this, check out Daniel Goleman's **Emotional Intelligence**, which makes a strong argument for the power of this skill to empower people.

"We judge ourselves by what we feel capable of doing, while others judge us by what we have already done," Henry Wadsworth Longfellow told us. Yes, yes, YES! And most of us tend to judge ourselves too harshly and take our mistakes and missteps too much to heart. When something like this happens, take deep breaths, clear your mind, and force yourself to engage in a diversionary activity, especially something physical as well as enjoyable.

A friend from Hong Kong came to visit Los Angeles and while we were driving around town, we chatted about our business activities. She managed multi-million-dollar properties in Sydney and in contrast, my business seemed, in comparison, rather small and insignificant. Being a typical, sharp-tongued, blunt Hong Kong type, she said to me, "You really don't know anything about what you are doing. Tsk, tsk."

Upon hearing her words, I actually felt my heart plummet down to my stomach and immediately felt devastated. For several days afterward, I was in a blue funk awash with feelings of insecurity, doubting my abilities and forgetting my achievements, and all the things I had accomplished up to that time, which actually, were considerable.

Then I began *thinking*, rather than *feeling*, enabling me to become less reactive to her frank comment. The more I thought about what she had said, the less dejected I felt, until it was not long until I had *thought* my way out of my disheartened state. The most important thing I did was to step back and look at the big picture, taking her tactless remark for what it was...exactly that.

I realized that in the grand scheme of things, she no longer had the power to hurt me. After all, she was really not a major or important person in my life or business, just a visitor, and her opinion was hers alone. It was imperative that I put *perspective* back into the picture; that in reality, nothing she could say or do could damage or detract from what I had already done, already accomplished, and recognized by people who I admired and respected.

You, too, need to develop that thick hide I mentioned earlier. There will be people who will be envious of your success and try to put or tear you down in order to make themselves feel or look good. It's called professional jealousy and there's a lot of it around in every field. Don't let those petty people subvert or undermine your confidence. There will be all sorts of reasons why they are doing it—envy, insecurity, laziness on their own part, inexperience, whatever.

It will happen to you as it did to me, but *choose* to rise above it by standing tall, knowing that *you* do not need to make someone else look or feel small to feel powerful and successful. Eleanor Roosevelt told us that no one can make us feel inferior without our consent and she was right. Nobody can take away the good things, deeds, and feelings that you have done or had.

Without faith in yourself and abilities, you will sabotage your dreams and your business. Self-esteem builds self confidence, success breeds success. Savor every success, no matter how small. Be kind and compassionate, especially to yourself. My cousin Dr. Annie Wong declared great words of wisdom once, "When all else fails, lower your standards!" I found it comforting and *forgiving* advice indeed for both of us who are over-achieving perfectionists. Remember, faith makes things possible, not easy.

Don't compare yourself with others, only with yourself. Glance backward occasionally to what you were doing a week, a month, or a year ago and take pride in how far along you've come. Competition is not necessarily bad, as it can stimulate you and your ideas, and energize your business. You don't have to prove anything to anyone but yourself. The only judge of your success is the one you see in the mirror.

You have a lot going for you, did you know that? The very fact that you are reading this book on entrepreneurship is testimony to your desire to succeed. Complacent, laid-back people do not concern themselves with self-improvement. Look around you at highly successful and prosperous role models and you will notice that you have much in common with them. Let *nothing* undermine you or your achievements. Avoid and ignore those naysayers who scoff at your ambitions and dreams.

Everything you have done up to now is a result of your hard work, patience, planning, and implementation. Have you ever counted all the details you took care of along the way, the number of telephone calls you made, books you read, people you met and networked with? Did you remember the forms you filled out, miles you have driven, supplies and equipment that you researched and purchased? When you start adding all of these things up, they amount to a lot, compared to what you started out with—just a dream.

You need to work on constantly reinforcing good feelings about yourself and what you have done. Be an optimist and expect good things as your due. Make a conscious effort to eliminate negative feelings and people who are "downers" from your life. Remove "I can't" and "But...." from your vocabulary. Listen to self-help tapes in your car and use affirmations and visualization to maintain a positive frame of mind and reference.

Stay motivated and on target, always keeping your destination, your goal, your dreams in sight. My husband taught me how to steer a sailboat to Catalina and to steer a car with the instruction, "Look at a point and always aim toward it." Never describe yourself and your company as a "small business." Such thinking limits your thinking and your potential. Rather, call yourself a "*growing* business" and your perception as well as that of those who hear it will change. You are what you *think* you are.

You are a very unique and special individual, unlike any other in the universe. How unique? Just start a list of your positive qualities and the things you have done or can do. Put everything, I mean *everything*, on the list, great and small, from being able to whistle to balancing your checkbook, from knowing how to program the VCR to blowing a bubble with gum, from swimming to cooking a turkey without burning it.

Think about things you usually don't think about, that you have never given yourself credit for, and that you may take for granted. Add to your list whenever you learn a new skill or how to do something in a different or creative way. You will be amazed and encouraged by your own individualism. No one else can do it like you do, and whenever you're feeling low, take the list out and look at it. Is there any doubt in your mind now that you are a valuable, capable person? Look how far you've come.

As you get older, you may discover, as I did, that giving to others is a great way to feel good about yourself. Since my college days when, as a junior at Virginia Polytechnic Institute, I was the founding president of Chi Delta Alpha, the university's first women's service sorority, I have found that helping other people boosts how I feel about myself. Try it, it works, over and over again. Then make this sharing of generosity and kindness to others a personal habit.

Share your resources with those less fortunate than yourself. Volunteer and discover how valuable and appreciated you are to those folks who have less in every way than you. As Jane Applegate advises: "When you're feeling depressed, give something away." I've followed her advice and it brought perspective about what is *really* important in life in some of my darker moments. Not surprisingly, it wasn't material things, power, fame, or money.

Aim for high standards and *reasonable, attainable* goals, those that you have a good chance of achieving. Don't set yourself up for a fall by setting impossible goals. Be honest and realistic about yourself, and what you can accomplish in an hour, a day, a week, or a month. Train yourself to maintain balance and harmony in your life and in everything that you do. Prioritize as to what's important and what's not and then be flexible if the situation changes and things don't go exactly as you planned, hoped, or expected. Much, as a matter of fact, *most* of what's in our lives is beyond our control. As an entrepreneur, you will need to learn to roll with the punches and take in stride whatever life deals you. Like a card or mah jong player, play with the hand you've been dealt, using all your skills to the best of your ability. As Eleanor Roosevelt said: "You have to accept whatever comes and the only important thing is that you meet it with courage and with the best you have to give."

What you *do* have total control over is your own performance, actions, and conduct, your integrity and your credibility, your reputation and your morals. Just accept responsibility for *your*self, *your* work, and *your* results and the other things will take care of themselves. *You* are the engineer of your destiny now as you embark upon your journey as an entrepreneur. Aristotle said it best: "We are what we repeatedly do. Excellence, then is not an act, but a habit."

The ability to separate the person that you are and your character from your business is essential, too. The ups and downs of your business experience *do not* reflect your character or competence. Acknowledge that life is not always fair, nor can we really understand why good people have bad experiences and are not always rewarded, and a lot of not so nice people seem to have things we aspire to having. Be wise and don't dwell on comparisons, for there will always be people in the world who are both more fortunate and less fortunate than you.

Be thankful for what you have and begin every day with a happy, hopeful heart. After all, you did wake up this morning, didn't you? Put a smile on your face and tell the image in the bathroom mirror, "I like myself and who I am. Today I will go forth and live the best day that I can." Then go out into the morning and savor every waking moment that you are alive. At the end of the day, go over what you accomplished and allow yourself to feel proud and satisfied for what you *did* do, whether it was one thing, or a hundred.

Here's the difference:

A winner says, "Let's find out."
A whiner says, "Nobody knows."

When a winner makes a mistake, he says, "It was my fault."
When a whiner makes a mistake, he says, "It wasn't my fault."

A winner makes a .
A whiner makes a promise.

A winner feels responsible for more than his job.
A whiner says, "That's not my department/job."

A winner says, "There ought to be a better way to do it."
A whiner says, "That's the way it's always been done."

A winner paces himself.
A whiner has only two speeds: hysterical and lethargic.

A winner says, "I'm good, but not as good as I ought to be."

A whiner says, "I'm not as bad as a lot of other people."

Into the Wild Blue Yonder

SECRET NUMBER 14

Opportunity

**When God closes a door, He opens a
window. I have always found views from
windows are far wider, brighter,
and better.**
-A.M. Wong

Ever since humankind began, it has tried to fathom why both good and bad things happen. The Chinese claim that everything in the universe is in a constant state of change and sacred *I Ching* described 64 possible conditions of flux. In contemporary Christian and other inspirational literature, theologians and laypeople alike attempt to explain the reasons. Are we somehow all a part of a universal grand plan orchestrated by someone or something beyond our comprehension? Who really knows, after all?

One thing I have found to be true is that a lot of things happen for the best. Perhaps you have experienced this, too. When something really awful happens, you probably feel pretty devastated. Later, as pain and disappointment fades with time, other things will occur that may lead you to believe that there was a reason for the occurrence in the first place. When life gives you lemons, not only make lemonade, but open up a stand and sell it!

Several years ago, the housing market in California took a nose dive and my intercultural consulting and training business slowed down proportionately. I thought it would be a good time to begin writing the manuscript for my book about understanding and targeting the U.S. Asian market. Participants in my workshops had expressed a desire to have their own copy of my materials instead of having to take many pages of notes.

I called Cynthia Chin-Lee, a longtime friend living in Northern California whose book on networking had been published in San Diego. She gave me the publisher's name and I sent an inquiry letter with ideas for sample chapters. Within two weeks, recognizing that the topic was a timely and "hot" one, he had offered me an author contract.

Being ignorant of how a book contract was constructed and unsure of my next move, I consulted a local friend who had authored several business books. He declared that I needed an agent and referred me to his. Mike Snell coached me on how to write the perfect book proposal and one revision later with high hopes and expectations, I made multiple copies to send to him. They were bound for the East Coast for consideration by several major publishers.

My summer was spent in a state of anticipation and anxiety, very much like the time when my husband and I waited for the approval of our home loan years before. Meanwhile, the San Diego contract waited on my desk as I continued to work on the manuscript and I waited for the results of Mike's efforts on my behalf. Finally, in September, I got word from him. I opened up my mailbox at the post office to find the entire stack of book proposals returned. The feeling of disappointment and failure was so painful as I unpacked them from their mailing envelope with the shredded newsprint that served as padding snowing all over the carpet.

By this time, the deadline for me to accept the San Diego contract had passed, and I had lost both the bird in my hand as well as those in the bush. For over a week, I felt a great sense of dejection and loss for what could have been. I knew in my heart that the book was important. After all, hadn't my agent Mike told me so in his brief note attached to the top copy of the returned proposals? He was sorry it didn't get picked up, he also wrote. I took the small piece of paper, taping it where I could see it every day.

In a later conversation, he explained that the consensus from the publishers was that they were very impressed with my background, loved my writing, but thought the subject was too narrow. One comment was that the book concept should have been broader, including other ethnic markets too, such as African American and Hispanic.

By the end of the week as the pain of crushed hopes and sharp disappointment began to fade, I had become philosophical about the rejections. Statistically, over 50,000 books were published each year, I discovered, and only *300* were bestsellers. Proven authors such as Danielle Steele, Stephen King, Erma Bombeck, V.C. Andrews, Michael Crichton, Jackie Collins, and Tom Chancey, of course, could expect seven-figure advances but unknown and untried writers were risky business. Publishing, after all, *is a business* and concerned with the bottom line. And then there were over 14,000 independent publishers in the country. Surely, I thought, at least one other than the fellow in San Diego would recognize the value of a landmark book on an unexplored topic.

As I continued to reflect, plan and plot strategies for making inquiries to prospective publishers, a feeling of urgency began to take hold. I was quite aware of the time it would take to query and wait, query and wait for responses from the companies. And if I had any thoughts about my book getting on the shelves any time soon, I knew well that the process of negotiating, editing, manufacturing, and marketing the book would take up to eighteen months or longer.

The more I thought about it, the less attractive it became to go that route. I agreed with my agent that the work was important, and I felt compelled to get it published as soon as possible so that businesses could benefit from its contents. It was then that I decided to create a company to independently publish **TARGET: The U.S. Asian Market,** *A Practical Guide to Doing Business*, and Pacific Heritage Books was born.

Working capital for PHB came from my well-established intercultural consulting and corporate training business, which by this time was four years old. The book made its debut just in time for the 1993 American Booksellers Association and American Library Association's annual conferences. Within six months, **TARGET** had sold out of its initial printing, gone into a second, broken even, and won *Bookdealer's World*'s Best Business Book of the Year Award.

I felt a tremendous sense of satisfaction when Mike called me a few months after the book had been published. An editor at one of the publishing companies had commented to him, "You know that little book on Asian American marketing that you brought to us? We should have picked it up." The icing on the cake came when *American Demographics* magazine accepted **TARGET** for its *Marketing Tools* catalog where it still remains, and the American Graduate School of Management

(Thunderbird) and other universities adopted it as a marketing text.

A year later Pacific Heritage Books, "proud publisher of Asian American titles," published **Night of the Red Moon,** my third book which was a historical fiction based on the Los Angeles Chinatown riot and massacre of 1871. This 96-page adventure for ages ten and older was favorably reviewed in length by the *Los Angeles Times Book Review* and caught the attention of the California Library Association. A letter came from a member of the John and Patricia Beatty Award committee requesting copies for consideration. The award honored children's literature that highlights California history and culture and I was thrilled at **Night of the Red Moon**'s nomination.

I continued to write and collaborated with Kirsten Lagatree on a book the subject of *feng shui*, the Chinese environmental art of placement, for Random House. **Feng Shui: Arranging Your Home to Change Your Life** was published in February, 1996, and Pacific Heritage Books promptly published **The Wind/Water Wheel:** *A Feng Shui Tool for Transforming Your Life* during the same summer. Mike Snell gave my name to Pam Gilberd who interviewed me for **11 Commandments of Wildly Successful Women** (Macmillan). In the coming year, my writing will appear in **The Feng Shui Anthology** and **The Marketing Yearbook**.

My successful and highly rewarding intercultural consulting and training business has evolved from a tiny spark after my cancer experience in 1989. Pacific Heritage Books was created when I encountered the roadblock of rejection in the fall of 1993. Both adverse experiences strengthened my character and resolve, and have directed me to great personal and professional growth, wonderful travels and adventures as well as meeting and making many new friends and clients. Without the misfortune, I never would have stretched and grown to become the businesswoman that I had always dreamed of being. Nor would I have been a guest on national television, radio, or the Oprah Winfrey Show.

These endeavors have brought me freedom, the true measure of success. Every one of these challenges forced me to think, strategize, organize, plan, and evolve. In other words, I had to *stretch*. Each summoned me to use my God-given gifts to make a difference in my life and community. All of them became successful through taking responsibility and risk. I truly believe that I am an ordinary person who has been able to do extraordinary things. Take a look around you and you will see that you are surrounded by others who did the same. Many of them are legendary now, especially those who are Olympic athletes who have overcome tremendous physical handicaps. But you don't have to look very far to find everyday heroes. Among the tops on my list of people I personally admire the most are single, working parents who are raising children.

You, too, will choose to do the same in establishing your business, and you, too, will get the credit for its success. Don't permit anything to get in the way of your achievements. No doubt there will be those who will discourage you or assail your dreams or efforts. As long as you keep the end in sight and your focus clear, nothing should deter you from setting goals and achieving them.

Owning and operating one's own business is not for the faint of heart. It does take much courage. Said Victoria, Queen of England, "Please understand there is no depression in this house and we are not interested in the possibilities of defeat. They do not exist."

SECRET NUMBER 15

Self Development

**Anyone who stops learning is old,
whether at twenty or eighty. Anyone
who keeps learning is young. The
greatest thing in life is to keep
your mind young.
-Henry Ford**

"How old would you be if you didn't know how old you are?" asked Satchell Paige. Have you ever met people who were young in years, but seemed very old? Do you notice that they were usually those who had become complacent, lazy, and had stopped bothering to learn? On the other hand, there are many elderly people who have stayed young at heart due to their love of learning new things. Everything around them brings excitement—new fashions, fads, technology, foods, cultures, languages, and ways of doing things. The difference is that the latter group stay young at heart by being actively *involved* in continuing self-development.

Ralph Waldo Emerson said it best: "There is no knowledge that is not power." Francis Bacon was more succinct: "Knowledge is power." Look around you and you will see that those who possess the most knowledge are those with the most power. In today's age of information and technology, this is even more true. Think of every wildly successful company that you know of or admire, whether it be a product or a service, low tech or high tech. Each one of these has access to the most current information in every aspect of its business, and *uses* it to forge its position in its particular market and beat out its competition.

How will *you* use the information that is available to you in libraries, on the Internet, on the Web, and an endless number of sources?

Without doing your homework, you should not start your business, for it is imperative to your success that you know as much as you can about every aspect before you embark on your entrepreneurial adventure. Remember that theories without a proper plan of action are useless. Be proactive in continuing education, for both yourself personally and for your business. It's just like being a train passenger; disembarking prevents you from reaching your destination.

To be on the cutting edge, you must have as much information as you can about every condition, external and internal, that affects your start-up. Ask yourself:

- What is your company's mission statement?
- What are your goals and objectives?
- What are the political, social, economic, and technological factors that will influence your business?
- What are your company's resources and capabilities?
- How do you and your company measure up to your competitors in terms of price and corporate structure, quality of product and service, sales, marketing, advertising, and public relations?
- Have you explored all opportunities and various market niches?
- Have you identified the market niches in which you will be most successful?

- How strong is your research and development department?
- How are you going about creating new products?
- What strategies are you planning and implementing?
- What are the timelines for facilitating them?
- What sort of monitoring system have you devised for all aspects for your business?
- What kind of customer feedback methods have been designed?
- How can you best collect from deadbeat customers, clients, and vendors?
- What are the best ways to deal with difficult customers?
- Which health or insurance plans are the most affordable and appropriate for you and your employees?

.....And so on.

"The secret of business is to know something that nobody else knows," said Aristotle Onassis. What do *you* know that nobody else knows? Do you have an inner radar for the right stock to buy before it takes off? Are you especially sensitive to the trends of electronic gadgetry? Perhaps you are particularly attuned to the needs of a special market? In the recent film **Twister**, the lead male character was described by one of his former colleagues as being a human barometer who could always predict accurately in which direction a certain tornado would move. We should all have at least a bit of that skill within each of us.

Just as I observed the demographic changes in Southern California over the twenty-some odd years during which I lived there and created a business niche from my research, you too, can be a vanguard in your chosen field. Read, watch, listen, and learn as much as you can. Learning is a treasure that no one can steal.

And yes, you can actually *feel* the power of your knowledge at work. Empowerment will come through knowledge about a wide range of things, not only how *much* you know but what you do with it. It is this same power that contributes much to energize, uplift, and enlighten your mental, spiritual, and emotional selves; in short, keep you alert of mind and young of heart.

"If it isn't growing, it's dying," Michael Gerber tells us. Physicians warn us that if you don't use it, you'll lose it and we are constantly reminded the same by piano teachers and physical therapists. It's true that muscles, for example, that are not used, atrophy, rending them weak and eventually, useless. When we do not use our intellect, won't it wither also? Just like a saw that needs constant sharpening to remain effective as a tool, our brainpower is the same. Or as Mom reminded us, practice makes perfect. From delivering a speech to mastering a computer language, from making a winning sales pitch to profitable negotiating, the more you exercise your business skills, the sharper they become. It's just like honing a knife.

The more you know, the more ready you will be to recognize opportunity when it knocks.   But don't be fooled, sometimes, opportunity doesn't make a grand, gaudy, or noisy entrance, but rather saunters by quietly and unobtrusively. Be sure to read at least one newspaper a day and several magazines a week, even if it is while you're standing in the line at the grocery store or post office after a long day at work! Keep informed about everything around you by staying alert to new, innovative ideas, products, processes, and other new businesses. Process information that you learn, hear, or read about and ask yourself how you can put it to use or what opportunities it creates.

Just today I answered the phone for Pacific Heritage Books and a woman inquired about the personalized books with children's names incorporated in the stories. As we were chatting, I suggested that she call her local library and find out if it had copies of magazines about home-based businesses and entrepreneurship. I myself had sent for a sample kit over a year ago after responding to an ad for such books in a magazine. The woman, who intimated that she was seventy years old and had a computer, became very excited when I suggested lightly that she could go into business creating those books herself.

"I belong to a church with over a thousand members," she told me.

"That's great," I said, "you have a built-in market right there!" Imagine if a chance phone call she made today launched her into a new, rewarding activity.

The Chinese believe that order came from chaos, and so it is that you may be able to notice or discern possibilities that other people have overlooked. Acknowledge that nothing stays the same, and that change is all around you. It is neither good or bad, it just *is*. How you deal with that change and adjust to it is a measure of your flexibility and maturity. A strong wind can knock down the mighty oak that doesn't bend, but the bamboo which arches and sways with the wind, allowing it to pass through its leaves and stalks, survives this mighty force of nature.

Like the bamboo, you can retain your identity and strength, even as the winds of change batter and blow. Don't just stand by and complacently accept the thinnest of excuses: "That's the way we've always done it." Can you come up with a new or different way of doing a task? Enlist the suggestions of those who have been doing the same job over and over. Surely through the years that person has given some thought as to how it could have been completed in another manner. Ask and you may be surprised. Encourage creative problem solving in your organization and establish an environment in which creative ideas are valued and nourished.

Knowledge gives you independence. The more research you conduct on your business, the less you have to rely on or pay someone else for that information, thus increasing both your effectiveness and profitability. Imagine how much we are willing to pay someone to give us information that we want but don't have. We spend billions annually on books, tapes, and videos, and to attend conferences, conventions, seminars, retreats, classes, and workshops—all in order to get more information.

Information keeps you competitive. Make it a policy to always keep updated as to what your competition is doing. You *do* know who your competition is, don't you? This should have been among the very first things you found out about your business before you started. Everything you can find out about the competition enables you to adjust your strategies accordingly. You can find out if your marketing is on target, or whether your pricing is comparable, too high or too low? You can also determine what products or services are *not* being provided and move to fill those unserved niches.

You can even win away your competitor's customers. How, you ask? Call them up and ask what services or products are they purchasing? From whom are they getting them? (Of course, you may already know the answer.) Is the customer satisfied with what he's getting? Is there something you can do for him or her that his/her present supplier or service-provider is not doing or is doing poorly? "Well," you say, "our company prides itself in _____, and I would be happy to help you eliminate the difficulties/frustration/dissatisfaction/etc. you've been experiencing. When would be a convenient time for me to come by to show you _____?" You are on your way!

Remember that journey of a thousand miles I mentioned at the beginning of this book? If you've reached this chapter, you have probably at least taken the first step. But experience is a valuable, although hard teacher. It gives the test before the class. Don't try to do everything at once. Take slow, prudent steps, making sure that your foot is on solid ground before taking the next. Deliberate often, a Latin proverb tells us, decide once. At least this way you will only have to back up a few steps if you make a misstep. Fools rushing in, where angels fear to tread, invariably end up too far in an unplanned direction. Correcting such careless mistakes may be very costly. Winston Churchill cautioned us: It is a mistake to look too far ahead. Only one link in the chain of destiny can be handled at a time.

Do not mistake high intelligence with automatic success, nor let yourself be "snowed" or intimidated by those who have more education than you. Having credentials, formal degrees, and expertise does not guarantee that a person is going to be an asset to your company, nor that he or she is going to do well on the job. As Daniel Goleman points out, it is those possessing the best human relations skills who are the most productive and effective in any organization.

Increasingly, workers who are a part of team with a common goal are becoming the norm in today's corporations. Their joint intelligence is higher when the individuals can synergize; their problem-solving skills are sharper. Conversely, the teams that are comprised of individuals who are socially inept and have not learned how to work effectively in tandem, are at a disadvantage. This emotional intelligence is the greater indicator of success later in life than high IQ scores.

If you remember, one of the first secrets of an entrepreneur is how well you know yourself. Here's something I learned to do at the first Wellness Community meetings I attended after I discovered that I had cancer. Make a list of all the things that make you happy. Tape it on your bathroom mirror or memorize it, and every day, try to do at least six things from the list. You will never be prosperous without being healthy. You cannot be healthy unless you are happy. You cannot be happy unless you have learned the secret of maintaining balance and harmony, the yin and yang, of both your personal and professional lives. Even if you only have done one or two things for yourself in a day, at least you did *something*, rather than nothing.

Doing something for *you* daily could be as simple as spending ten minutes savoring quiet moments and a cup of tea or coffee or chatting with someone you love or as invigorating as your hour-long morning walk or pounding the racquetball at the fitness center. It may be an activity that is a no-brainer or escapist, or it may be something intellectually stimulating totally unrelated to your work. It may be taking the time to pray or meditate. Whatever you choose, it will the right choice for you. Only you and you alone know how best to recharge your inner self, the essence that is uniquely you...your spirit and your soul.

Knowing how to nourish your mind, body, and soul is as essential to the welfare of your entrepreneurial venture as are the technical and practical information you possess. I believe it is *the* most important element, just like the brain and the central nervous system is to your body. Making that time for yourself is giving value to the person that you are. It tells you daily that *you are important*. It builds your self-esteem and self-confidence. Most of all, it creates your *center*.

Your center is the place within you that is the core of your strength. Once you have achieved the state of centeredness, you will be solid, stable, and unshakable. You will have found *who* you really are, know *what* you are, *where* you are, and in this state, have truly discovered your mission in life. Not surprisingly, the journey that you took, will have guided you to meet your destiny. Not surprisingly, that same journey will have guided you back to Secret Number 2.

You will instantly know when you have reached this pinnacle of fulfillment. It happens when you feel the cups of your mind, body, and spirit running over. It will give you an incredible sensation and sense of well-being and peace. It is a wonderful feeling of being totally in touch with yourself and your life. It is a feeling of contentment, happiness, satisfaction and achievement. It is peace of mind and peace of heart. And interestingly enough, when you have achieved it, you will find that it has absolutely nothing to do with money, fame, or prestige, and everything to do with power—*YOURS!*

SECRET NUMBER 16

Passing on the Torch

**One thing I know: The only ones among
you who will be truly happy are those
who will have sought and found how
to serve.**
-Albert Schweitzer

There are many paths to the top of the mountain, but the view is still the same. I hope that you have been enjoying the journey, learning much along the way, stopping often and to rest to appreciate the view and the progress you've made. Whether you've reached the summit or are still travelling, take a moment to reflect on how far you've progressed. Give yourself a pat on the back. You've come a long way, baby, up the peaks and down in the valleys. Know that without the serenity and quiet of the valleys, you could not ascend to the summits of the mountains. But you had staying power and are a winner. After all, you *knew* that winners never quit and quitters never win.

Close your eyes and think back to the day you caught the entrepreneurial spirit, the proverbial lightbulb went on in your head, or that special moment when you told yourself that you were ready to commit to your venture. Play the memories back through your mind like a video and recall the early days, months, or years when you were perhaps tinkering or crammed into your garage or in the spare bedroom or even on the dining table. (Don't scoff at businesses that operate out of garages, remember that some of the world's most profitable, technological companies had humble beginnings, too.) Think about those moments of self-doubt, of indecision, of small successes, of big steps that took lots of heart and even more courage. Remember when...?

As the recollections come into your mind's view, which faces appear? Who were the people who were there for you, giving you love, friendship, moral support, financial assistance, and the wisdom of their years and experience? Now freeze the frame and remember those folks—your husband, wife, parents, in-laws, relatives, friends, mentors, business associates, acquaintances, teachers, professors, neighbors, fellow members from the chamber of commerce and civic organizations, and everyone else. Don't ever forget those folks because without their encouragement and support, you probably wouldn't have come this far, wherever you are now

And now it's *your* turn to give back. Payback time, kiddo.

Start with small, random acts of kindness that cost absolutely nothing. Could you just say thank you to six people a day, whether you know them or not? It may be the checker at the supermarket, a cheerful bus driver, or a harried sales clerk. It could just be telling your son or daughter that you noticed that she loaded the dishwasher or he made his bed without your asking to do so. Once you get into the habit, take the second step.

Look just a little bit farther out to those with whom you associate or work daily. Could you take just one person who works for you under your wing and give a little extra support or encouragement, a word of praise? Could you give an employee, associate, or colleague, or anyone you know just a few extra minutes of your time? Mentoring doesn't take very much when it's done close to you.

Don't be stingy with your time if you have some to give. Don't be stingy with your money if you have some to give. Don't be stingy with your passion, your enthusiasm, your wisdom, if you have some to give. I have found that if you always give, you will always have, whatever it is—love, attention, kindness, and all the other good things in life.

Now expand the circle once more and look into the community. From your alma mater to local civic groups, there will be countless opportunities for you to give something back. Many non-profit organizations are dedicated to charity or service. Choose any that are close to your heart or interests. Be sure to include at least one group that furthers the success of individuals, especially those having to do with business start-ups, and especially include young people or those who may have been overlooked or fallen through the cracks of the system.

Don't forget that once upon a time, *you* were standing at the threshold, uncertain and nervous, full of heart and hope. Someone ahead on the road turned around, saw you, and waited for you to catch up and gave you guidance and support. Perhaps it wasn't a road but the corporate ladder you were climbing. Still, there was someone very special, who took the time to look back at you and leaned down to give you a hand up.

One of my mentors was Lynne Choy Uyeda. We met years ago when we were both volunteering as announcers for Chinese New Year stage performances in Chinatown, and with whom I had lost contact. At a Chinese New Year banquet in

1989, we met again after *eighteen* years. Finding this particular friend again was like finding a treasure, and that she was.

As the principal of one of the pioneer Asian American public relations firms in the United States, Lynne encouraged me to start my own business that spring, just a few months before I discovered that I had cancer. Big of heart and generous in spirit, she was a shoulder to lean on, a sympathetic ear, and unwavering moral support as I traveled the entrepreneurial path.

To know the road ahead, ask those coming back. I asked Lynne as well as others who had the wisdom and experience that I lacked. Almost always, somebody somewhere found the time for me. Even with their lofty titles and busy schedules, these supporters gave me advice and good counsel when I needed it, and I will never forget their kindness.

For you and me, it's much like passing on a torch to those who are travelling the same road and need a guiding light in order to see. Take the time to discover what that person's destination is and give your assistance for him or her to reach it. Being an empathetic listener may be all he or she needs. Everyone has something to share, including you. Share what you do best.

If you give a man a fish, he will eat for a day. If you teach a man to fish, he will eat for a lifetime. Teach what you have learned. Pass on what you know. I have a variation of Francis Bacon's "Money is like muck—not good unless it be spread." Mine goes: Knowledge is most beneficial when you spread it around. Be a role model. Give time to those who need you. If you can't give time, give money or other resources to individuals and organizations that support self-development and self-reliance. If you can't give those, at least give hope. Share your mission. Inspire a young or older person. Stretch out your hand or arms and touch someone. In the process you will find that doing so will make you feel rich and rewarded.

True greatness in a person is the ability to make you feel that you can be great too. I can't take credit for saying that, but I believe in it wholeheartedly. Many people are impressed with all that I've accomplished, that I have appeared on the Oprah Winfrey Show or any number of other national television features. I tell them that those experiences were great adventures and a lot of fun. Like Andy Warhol said: "Everyone gets fifteen minutes of fame." I don't mind getting my fifteen minutes' worth, but I only want to experience them, thirty seconds at a time throughout my life in order to savor them!

You don't need me to tell you that you're something special. You've already proved that on your own. Can't you *feel* the satisfaction when you've made someone else feel that way too? Doesn't it feel *fabulous*? You may never know which seeds of kindness, charity, faith, compassion, encouragement, or hope you scattered will take root and flourish.

Four instances stand out in my mind.

I was raised in a three-generation household in which my paternal grandparents were my role models, dedicating their lives to service to their country and fellow men. There was never any question that I too, would be involved in my community as I grew up in Taiwan, but I did not really get a chance to do something until after my high school graduation.

In 1964, I entered Virginia Polytechnic University located in Blacksburg, Virginia, a five hour-ride by Greyhound bus from my home in Washington, D.C. I was asked to become the copy editor of the university's yearbook, *The Bugle*, and accepted the position. During the following two years, I was the editor-in-chief.

Although being on the yearbook staff taught me many new skills that were to become valuable later in my life, it did not satisfy my yearning to contribute something to the community. I did notice, however, that although the university had many campus organizations for its approximately 5,000 male and 300 female students, there was not one for women dedicated to community service.

For a university whose motto was "Ut Prosim," translated into English from Latin as "That I May Serve," I found that deficiency puzzling. During my junior year, a group of my friends and I took steps to form a women's service organization at Virginia Tech. On February 22, 1967, Chi Delta Alpha was chartered as the first and only women's service organization in Virginia Polytechnic Institute's history. Two months later in April, the twelve charter members initiated twenty-six new sisters in service. And in June, I, the founding president of the group, left the university to marry and to transfer to the University of Southern California in Los Angeles.

Skip twenty years to 1987. Twenty years have passed since my departure from Tech and I am now a long-married wife, mother of four, and a professional educator in Southern California. One day I open my mailbox at my home in Palos Verdes and find a small envelope among the bills and junk mail.

Imagine my astonishment and surprise to find an announcement which reads:

The Sisters of Chi Delta Alpha
cordially invite you to participate
in the celebration of their twentieth anniversary
on the 30th of May, Nineteen hundred and eighty-seven
at the Sheraton Red Lion Inn, Blacksburg, Virginia
Eight o'clock p.m. to one o'clock a.m.

I remember feeling faint with shock of it. I read and reread the invitation a dozen times, not believing what I had received and the significance of it. The modest piece of stationery that I held in my shaking hands meant that the organization that I had helped to establish two decades before had survived the test of time.

Incredibly, Chi Delta Alpha was operational, thriving, and still serving the rural community of southern Virginia for all those years. To be truthful, I had never given a thought to it after I left Tech, having been too busy adjusting to a new life as a bride and transfer student on the West Coast. It was just one of those seeds I had sown and not only taken root, but had grown to become a great tree that was benefiting its surrounding environment. The discovery just blew me away!

The second incident came as a call from Chicago from a complete stranger about nine months after the publication of **TARGET**. The voice on the phone was from a Chinese-American woman who was delighted to reach me. Thanking me profusely, she told me that it was due to the reading of my book that she had decided to write her doctoral dissertation on the subject of Asian American marketing. Once again, I was absolutely stunned that something I had done had made such a difference in someone's life. I was dumbfounded.

The last two instances were a developer who had heard me speak at a luncheon and used one idea I suggested during my speech. He later reported that his home sales "went through the roof" to over ten million dollars.

Last, but not least, is the story of Mae Ling Wong who learned the proper way to present a business card at a workshop sponsored by the Asian Professional Exchange and other organizations last year. I ran into her recently and she told me that she had attended a regional meeting for Apple Computer International in Asia shortly thereafter. Mae Ling thanked me profusely.

"I was one of the few women there," she explained, giving me a huge smile and a big hug. "I was so proud that I knew how to bow, shake hands, and especially to present my business card among all the Japanese. I got a promotion and am now the Developer Program Manager in Asia," she said, correctly presenting her new business card to me in perfect form.

Keep on sowing those seeds. Some of them will fall on cement or infertile soil. Others will be carried away by the wind. Still others may sprout but not grow to maturity. But many will take root and create a beautiful new plant and *you* will have contributed to its life and development.

Have you ever seen some of the seeds that come in colorful paper packets at the plant nurseries and home improvement stores in the middle of winter? They are tiny, just the mustard seed, for example. We, too, are like those seeds. And yet within every single little one is all the material essential for it to develop into a blossoming plant that will brighten up someone's world. For that seed to reach its potential, it needs nutrients, sunlight, water, air, and attention. Even the mightiest oak originates from a little acorn the size of a small pebble.

Your business begins from a delicate wisp of dreams to evolve into something very special and unique, just like the entrepreneur you are. It may be a one-person sole proprietorship or a multi-billion-dollar global conglomerate. Whatever form it takes, it represents *your* courage and hard work, stamina and energy, passion and perseverance, ingenuity and ideas, intelligence and resourcefulness, the many risks you take and the responsibilities that you were and still are willing to tackle.

You've done well, kiddo. Hold your head a bit higher. Stand a little taller. Give yourself a pat on the back and take the day off. You deserve it. Your community, country, and world need more exceptional, talented, imaginative, and visionary people like you. And keep up the good work. You're a winner.

Appendix

Writing a Business Plan

To whomever you approach to fund your business start-up, you will need to prepare a business plan. Use the following form to develop your business plan. As you research its various aspects, modify, revise, or refocus accordingly. The entire plan should be approximately two to three pages in length maximum and have the following components:

I. Executive Summary
    A. Mission Statement

II. Table of Contents

III. Business Concept
    A. How did you arrive at the concept for your
       business?
    B. What makes your service or product unique?
    C. Who or what is your competition?
    D. What facts have your researched to support
       interest or viability of this concept?

IV. Company Description
    A. What is your principal product or service?
    B. What are the factors that give you a competitive

advantage?

V. Market Analysis
    A. Provide an overview of the industry you are entering
    B. What is its size?
    C. What are its current and projected trends?
    D. What is the industry's anticipated potential for growth?
    E. How will the seasons affect your business?
    F. What local, regional, or global economic conditions will affect your industry and business?

VI. Market Plan
    A. Who/What is your market for this product/service?
    B. How will it be distributed
    C. What is the pricing structure?
    D. How will sales be handled?
    E. What sort of advertising will you do for it?
    F. What promotions do you have planned?
    G. How will the product be packaged?
    H. What are your sales projections?
    I. Who are your sales personnel?

VII. Manufacturing
    A. At what facilities will your product be manufactured?

B. Describe the research, design and development
   of your product.
C. What plans do you have to reduce, reuse, and
   recycle?

VIII. Operations
    A. Describe the following day-to-day operations
   of your business:
        1. Key operations staff
        2. Control
        3. Collections
        4. Shipping
        5. Invoicing
        6. Bookkeeping
        7. Other

IX. Management
    A. Provide the biographies and resumes of the key
   managers.
    B. How will recruitment of new staff be handled?
    C. What kinds of incentive plans are there?
    D. Who is on your board of directors and what
   functions will they perform?
    E. Who will be the current stockholders in the
   business?
    F. Who is on the organizational chart and what are
   their responsibilities?

G. What kind of business is this: sole proprietorship, general partnership, limited partnership,
corporation, S corporation, or ?

X. Personnel
A. What job positions will be filled in preparation
for your grand opening?
B. What are the job requirements for those
positions?
C. What are the employee qualifications?
D. What are the wage and salary requirements?
E. What plans do you have for background checks
on applicants?
F. What plans do you have for creating a diverse
staff?
G. What plans do you have for training and
orientation?
H. What evaluation processes do you have in
place?
I. What criteria have been established for bonuses,
salary increases, commissions, promotions,
etc.?
J. How will job performance be assessed and
recorded?
K. How will issues of sexual harassment,
discrimination, race-motivated actions, etc. be
handled and resolved?

XI. Strategic Growth Plan

A. What short and long-term growth plans do you have?

B. What plans do you have for diversifying your business?

XI. Funding Requirements

    A. What are your immediate financing requirements/needs?

    B. What are your funding requirements for the next five years?

    C. Give an itemized list of fund usage.

    D. What are the terms of investment?

XII. Financial Data

    A. What are the financial projections for your business?

    B. Give the monthly profit and loss figures for first year.

    C. Give the proforma profit and loss projections

    D. What is your anticipated cash flow?

    E. Provide a balance sheet for the first five years.

XIII. Permits and Licenses

    A. Business License (city)

    B. Business License (state)

    C. Legislation regarding home-based businesses

    D. Fictitious Name Statement

    E. Sales Tax Permit

    F. Federal identification number

G. State Employment Tax

XIV. Compliance with Local, State and Federal Laws
    A. Federal identification number
    B. Americans with Disabilities Act of 1990
    C. Family and Medical Leave Act of 1993
    D. ERISA requirements
    F. OSHA guidelines
    G. Fair Labor and Standards Act
    H. Other laws, e.g. anti-discrimination, immigration, Social Security, medical, dental, vision insurance, recycling, hazardous material disposal, composting, etc.

XV. Location
    A. Leasing
    B. Renting
    C. Remodeling
    D. Purchasing
    E. Other options
    F. Crime
    G. Visibility
    H. Office space
    I. Manufacturing space
    J. Storage space
    K. Shipping and mailing
    L. Packing
    M. Loading dock
    N. Parking

O. Handicap access and parking

P. Restrooms

Q. Energy costs

R. Utilities

S. Zoning

T. Proximity to population, police, fire, civic
   centers, etc.

U. Proximity to skilled and unskilled labor pool

XVI. Patents and Copyrights
   A. Has your patent or copyright been applied for?

XVII. Income Taxes

XVIII. Bookkeeping System

XIX. Insurance

XX. Appendices
   A. Collateral material to support you business plan
      including photographs, specifications, market
      research, data, census information, letters of
      intent, etc.

XXI. Grand Opening
   A. Media release/announcement
   B. Invited guests/potential customers/suppliers
      city officials/friends/neighboring
      businesses/etc.

C. Caterer

D. Photographer

E. Planning and implementation

F. Florist

G. Chamber of commerce (ribbon cutting?)

H. Promotions/advertisements in media

I. Framing of photographs, clippings

Many excellent materials have been written about starting your own businesses. Investigate these useful books, kits, tapes, and courses available to you.

Bibliography

Aburdene, Patricia and Naisbitt, John. *Megatrends for Women.*
New York: Villard Books, 1992
-Megatrends 2000. New York: Villard Books, 1990.

Adams, Bob. Small Business Startup. Holbrook, Massachusetts:
Adams Media Group, 1996.

Alessandra, Tony and O'Conner, Michael J. with VanDyke,
Janice. *People Smart: Powerful Techniques for Turning
Every Encounter into a Mutual Win.* La Jolla, California:
Keynote Publishing Company, 1990.

Applegate, Jane. *Succeeding in Small Business: The 101
Toughest Problems and How to Solve Them.* New York:
Plume Books, 1992.

Blout, Elkan, editor. *The Power of Boldness.* Washington, D.C.:
Joseph Henry Press, 1996.

Boutiller, Robert. *Targeting Families: Marketing to and Through
the New Family.* Ithaca, New York: American
Demographics Books, 1993.

Clancy, Kevin J. and Shulman, Robert S. *Marketing Myths That
Are Killing Business: The Cure for Death Wish
Marketing.* New York: McGraw-Hill, 1994.

Covey, Stephen R. *The 7 Habits of Highly Effective People*. New York: Fireside, 1989.

Daily, Frederick. *Tax Savvy for Small Business*. Berkeley: Nolo Press, 1996.

Deep, Sam and Sussman, Lyle. *Yes, You Can!* Reading, MA: Addison-Wesley Publishing, 1996.

Dell, Donald L. *Minding Other People's Business: Winning Big for Your Clients and Yourself.* New York: Villard Books, 1989.

DeVries, Henry and Gage, Diane. *Self-Marketing Secrets: Winning by Making Your Name Known.* San Marcos, California: Avant Books, 1991.

Entrepreneur Magazine. *Starting A Home-Based Business*. New York: John Wiley, 1996.

Gerber, Michael. *The E Myth*. New York: HarperCollins, 1987.

Gilberd, Pamela Boucher. *The Eleven Commandments of Wildly Successful Women*. New York: Macmillan Spectrum, 1996.

Goleman, Daniel. *Emotional Intelligence*. New York: Bantam, 1995.

Hakuta, Ken. *How to Create Your Own Fad and Make a Million Dollars*. New York: Avon Books, 1988.

Halloran, James W. *Why Entrepreneurs Fail*. Liberty Hall Press, 1991.

Hill, Napolean. *Think and Grow Rich*. New York: Fawcett Columbine, 1988.

Korda, Michael. *Success!* New York: Ballantine Books, 1977.

Leeds, Dorothy. *Marketing Yourself: The Ultimate Job Seeker's Guide*. New York: HarperCollins*Publishers*, 1991.

Maas, Jane. *Better Brochures, Catalogs, and Mailing Pieces*. New York: St. Martin's Press, 1981.

Ortlund, Anne and Ray. *You Don't Have to Quit*. Nashville, Tennessee: Thomas Nelson Publishers, 1986, 1988.

Ries, Al and Trout, Jack. *The 22 Immutable Laws of Marketing: Violate Them at Your Own Risk!* New York: HarperBusiness, 1993.

Robbins, Anthony. *Giant Steps: Small Changes to Make a Big Difference-Daily Lessons in Self Mastery*. New York: Simon and Schuster, 1994.

Roger-John and McWilliams, Peter. *You Can't Afford the Luxury of a Negative Thought.* Los Angeles: Prelude Press, 1988, 1989.

Smith, Brian R. Smith. *How to Become Successfully Self-Employed.* Holbrook, Mass.: Bob Adams Inc. Publishers, 1991, 1993.

Smith, Jeanette. *The Publicity Kit: A Complete Guide for Entrepreneurs, Small Businesses and Nonprofit Organizations.* New York: John Wiley and Sons, Inc. 1991.

Waitley, Denis. *Seeds of Greatness: The Ten Best-Kept Secrets of Total Success.* Old Tappan, New Jersey: Fleming H. Revell Company, 1983.

Waldrop, Judith with Mogelonsky, Marcia. *The Seasons of Business: The Marketer's Guide to Consumer Behavior.* Ithaca, New York: American Demographics Books, 1992.

Walton, Donald. *Are You Communicating? You Can't Manage Without It.* New York: McGraw-Hill, 1989.

Index

winner, 70, 128, 175, 176, 203
Wong, Dr. Annie, 171
word of mouth, 61, 66, 109, 137, 139, 140
Word of mouth, 141

About the Author

The daughter of a diplomat and industrialist, Angi Ma Wong was born in Nanking, China, and lived in New Zealand, Taiwan, and Washington, D.C. In 1967, as a junior at Virginia Polytechnic Institute, she founded Chi Delta Alpha, the first and only women's service sorority at the university, which in 1997, celebrated its thirtieth anniversary. Ms. Wong later graduated from the University of Southern California with a B.A. in English, and completed post-graduate studies at California State University at Long Beach, and at the University of California at Los Angeles.

In 1989, she coined the title of *intercultural consultant* and founded her intercultural consulting and corporate training services, and Pacific Heritage Books in 1993, both dedicated to bridging cultures for better business. Since then, she has created and secured a niche as a pioneer and internationally-recognized authority on the U.S. Asian market.

Through consulting, seminars, training, public speaking, writing, and publishing, Angi Ma Wong facilitates profitability between Asians and non-Asians globally. Her diverse and impressive clientele includes over sixty major residential and commercial developers nationwide, as well as architectural and interior design firms, AT & T, Bank of America, New York Life Insurance, First Interstate Bank, the U.S. Fish and Wildlife Service, Home Savings of America, cities, retailers, and school districts.

Ms. Wong is an award-winning businesswoman and author. In 1995, she was honored as an Outstanding Los Angeles Businesswoman of the Year by the National Association of Women Business Owners (NAWBO). Merrill Lynch and Ernst and Young co-nominated Ms. Wong for INC. magazine's prestigious Entrepreneur of the Year award.

Angi Ma Wong's landmark **TARGET:** *The U.S. Asian Market, A Practical Guide to Doing Business*, was the first book written on designing, marketing, and selling to Asians on both sides of the Pacific. It won the Best Business Book of the Year from *Bookdealers World*. Her historical fiction, **Night of the Red Moon,** based on the 1871 Los Angeles Chinatown riot and massacre, was favorably reviewed in *the Los Angeles Times, Asian Week*, and the *International Examiner*. The book was nominated for the John and Patricia Beatty award for children's literature.

Ms. Wong has also authored **The Wind/Water Wheel:** *A Feng Shui Tool for Transforming Your Life* (Pacific Heritage Books, 1996), **The Practical Feng Shui Chart Kit:** *A Tool to*

Chart the Direction of Your Life (Pacific Heritage Books, 1992), and **Sane Motherhood** (1982). She served as the advisor to Kirsten Lagatree's **Feng Shui:** *Arranging Your Home to Change Your Life* (Random House, 1996) and wrote its foreword. Ms. Wong is a contributing author **to The Feng Shui Anthology** (Earth Design, 1997), and **The Marketing Yearbook** (Prentice Hall, 1997). She was featured in Pam Gilberd's **11 Commandments of Wildly Successful Women** (MacMillan, 1996).

Angi Ma Wong has been interviewed on OPRAH, *USA Today* (she is a member of its Baby Boomer panel), *New York Times, Los Angeles Times, Seattle Times, Chicago Tribune, Asian Week, Trade and Culture, YOLK, TRANSPACIFIC.* She and her work have been feaured on CBS, ABC, NBC, FOX-TV, and on national and international radio. Several of her letters to the editor have been published in *TIME*.

She resides in Palos Verdes, California, with her husband Norman, and their children: Jason, Wendy, Jamie, and Steven.

PACIFIC HERITAGE BOOKS
Order Form

Quan.

____**Been There, Done That**: *16 Secrets of Success for Entrepreneurs* * @ $14.95 each....................$_____

____**TARGET: The U.S. Asian Market**, *A Practical Guide to Doing Business* * @ $27.50 each.........$_____

____**The Practical** *Feng Shui* **Chart Kit**: *A Tool for Charting the Direction of Your Life*@ $29.95..$_____

____**The Wind/Water Wheel**: *A Feng Shui Tool for Transforming Your Life* * @ $19.95 each...$_____

____**Night of the Red Moon** * @ $16 each.............$_____

____**The Feng Shui Anthology** @ $27.50.............$_____

____**Feng Shui**: *Arranging Your Home to Change Your Life* @ $14.95.....................................$_____

Subtotal $_____

Calif. residents add 8.25% sales tax $_____

All orders add 10% shipping & handling $_____

Circle one: Check VISA MC M.O. for the total of $_____

Name_____

Address_____

City_____Zip_____

Credit Cardholder name _____

Signature_____Exp. Date_____

Acct. No._____

*Can be autographed by A.M. Wong: Which books and to whom would you like them personalized? Send total payment to: Pacific Heritage Books, Box 3967-BTBB, Palos Verdes, CA 90274-9547, fax your order to (310)541-7178, or call toll-free to 1-888-870-8878.